Myths of
Social Media

Myths of Social Media

Dismiss the misconceptions and use social media effectively in business

Michelle Carvill
Ian MacRae

KoganPage

First published in Great Britain and the United States in 2020 by Kogan Page Limited

2nd Floor, 45 Gee Street
London
EC1V 3RS
United Kingdom

122 W 27th St, 10th Floor
New York, NY 10001
USA

4737/23 Ansari Road
Daryaganj
New Delhi 110002
India

www.koganpage.com

ISBNs

Hardback   978 0 7494 9873 3
Paperback   978 0 7494 9871 9
Ebook   978 0 7494 9872 6

British Library Cataloguing-in-Publication Data

A CIP record for this book is available from the British Library.

Library of Congress Control Number

2020931757

Typeset by Integra
Print production managed by Jellyfish
Printed and bound by CPI Group (UK) Lid, Croydon CR0 4YY

For Marques and Jaiden Lui
So I heard you like Mudkips?

Josephine and Eliza, your mumma is back (for a while!) ;)

CONTENTS

MYTH 1

SOCIAL MEDIA IS A WASTE OF TIME

Before assuming that social media is always a waste
of time, ask the questions 'What do I want to achieve?'
and 'Can social be used to help me achieve that goal?'

Introduction

Is social media a waste of time? A study by Pew Research found that 82 per cent of Americans thought so.[1] However, that doesn't mean they're staying away from it. The same study reported that more people are now getting their news information from social media than from print media.

The majority of people, however, do use social media, irrespective of whether they think it is a good use of time. Pew reported that in 2019, 79 per cent of the US population had a social media profile, while 11 per cent didn't use the internet at all.[2] The number of social media users is lower in the UK – while 90 per cent of the population have internet access, the Office for National Statistics suggests just 65 per cent use social media.[3]

All this is to say that: if social media is a waste of time, it has not stopped people from using it.

People waste time at work

It is necessary to distinguish between using social media for business or personal use. If someone spends most of their time after work scrolling through Facebook or Twitter, it is up to them to judge whether or not that time is wasted. However, if they spend time during their workday on personal social media to pass the time, or have private conversations, that almost certainly is time wasted if there is something else they ought to be doing.

Of course, there can be a bit of a grey area between personal social media use and work-related networking or 'fact finding' missions. But, if someone feels the need to make an excuse for why they have been spending work hours on their personal social media, they probably were wasting time.

If the question was 'Do people waste time on social media?' the answer would certainly be a resounding yes. But this problem is not unique to social media. There are few, if any, technologies, activities or tools that you can provide people without them finding a way to waste time with it. Give the right person the right distraction, and you'll never hear from them again. Even time management software can be a waste of time: some people spend more time organizing and sprucing up their to-do lists than completing the tasks on the list.

People can waste time on social media at work, or anywhere at any time with the help of a smartphone with an internet connection. People can waste time watching TV, in the break room, on their phones. Even without any external distractions, employees can spend their time daydreaming instead of working.

There is nothing wrong with switching off from work – it is great to be able to when the time is appropriate and people will choose their own distractions and decide for themselves whether or not these are a good or bad use of time.[4] But for the purpose of this chapter and much of this book, we want to discuss social media in the context of productivity and performance at work.

Yes, people can waste their own and their employer's time on social media at work – but there are also many ways in which social media can be a good use of time at work, and can actually be used to improve productivity, engagement and communication (Chapter 13) sales (Chapter 16), recruitment (Chapters 22 and 23) and customer relations (Chapter 12 and 15).

Above all, we need to recognize that there are perils and pitfalls to social media use – so we will be explaining what to watch out for, what to avoid and what to be cautious of in the subsequent chapters. All applications of social media have risks as well as benefits. So before assuming that social media is always a waste of time, ask the questions 'What do I want to achieve?' and 'Can social be used to help me achieve that goal?' With a bit of knowledge and creativity, it's amazing what can be accomplished using social media – just ask the Kremlin (see Chapter 7)!

Weighing the benefits, risks and costs

The uses for social media at work are as varied as the business activities within and between companies. Some companies use social media for sales and marketing (Chapters 8 and 10), others use it for recruiting new talent (Chapter 23) and others have their own internal social networks (Chapter 13).

Just because people waste time on computers or smartphones or social media, that doesn't mean that the technology is inherently a time-waster. If you're considering allowing the use of social media at work, instead of making vague generalizations, think about the specifics of how the technology will be used, and for what:

- **Purpose**. What is the technology going to be used for, and why? The purpose must be established upfront, and all subsequent issues can be weighed against how suitable the technology is for its purpose.

- **Availability**. Who is the technology available to? Is it publicly available, or are there significant barriers to using it? Is it cost-effective and user-friendly enough for your business, employees or customers?

- **Fitness for purpose**. How well does the technology fit with the purpose identified above? Some technologies fit well enough, and some can be adapted. However, if the technology doesn't fit with the intended purpose or business outcomes, it could be a waste of time.

- **Reliability**. How reliable is the technology? If there are frequent outages, technical problems or constant changes that make it unreliable, it may not be very useful.

- **Maturity**. How well-developed is the technology? Advanced and well-tested systems tend to be more reliable and better developed to specific purposes. More popular platforms also tend to be easier for employees and customers to adopt because of their familiarity.

- **Provenance.** How reputable is the technology or platform, who is the developer, and in which country is it based? For professional social networking, for example, established platforms and developers may be a better fit than obscure online forums.

- **Support**. Does the platform or technology provide the necessary implementation and maintenance support? Is there anyone to contact if something goes wrong? If a company decides to outsource the communication, their networking, their performance management systems or similar processes to an external platform, there must be appropriate support available.

- **Scalability**. Does the platform have the capacity to support your current and future requirements? It may be reasonable to move to a different platform if your requirements change, but it's wise to consider this in advance.

- **Usability**. How easy and accessible is the platform for users? Introducing clunky, inefficient or confusing platforms may be counterproductive and lead to wasted time.

- **Costs**. What are the potential costs (financial or otherwise) of using the technology and platform? If the purpose is clearly defined, the potential rewards (again, financial or otherwise) should be clear and can then be measured against costs.

- **Risks**. What potential problems come with using the technology? There may be risks for the company's reputation or that of its employees, risks associated with customer data or with potential misuse of the platform. These frequently lead to unforeseen costs.

- **Utility**. Overall, how do all of these points add up? After weighing costs, risks and benefits against the purpose, it is possible to estimate the overall utility of the platform. Overall, is it worth using, or is there a better way of accomplishing the stated purpose?

Take the example of a company using a platform that is both an internal company social media network and a performance management system (this will be discussed in more detail in Chapter 13). Its purpose is to be an internal communication network for employees, which lets individuals track their own performance, while allowing colleagues to provide feedback and managers to track and record progress. There should be different levels of private, partially private and public information.

There are specific platforms that do exactly this. However, some of the more well-known social media platforms such as Facebook or LinkedIn might provide some of those features, but not all. The low cost and potential for scalability might be in these platforms' favour, but their fitness, risks and overall utility may not measure up.

These 12 factors may not all be equally important to you, depending on the platform's purpose, so in many cases it will make sense to focus on a few. For example, smaller businesses may want to test out new systems while prioritizing costs and reliability. Factors such as provenance and scalability may be less important in the short term.

The key message to remember is that anything can be a waste of time when it is used incorrectly. It takes a little more effort to ascertain whether a certain platform has the potential to be valuable, and if it matches up with the purpose for which you need it.

Opting out of social media

Do you still think social media is a complete waste of time? That's fine – you can always choose to opt out. But even if you have no desire to participate in anything related to social networking in the workplace, you should still read this book and understand how other people and companies are using it.

Perhaps you believe that social media is all well and good, has varied uses and benefits, but you just do not want to share any of your personal data with tech behemoths, internet service providers and/or corporate HQ. That's a perfectly reasonable option that some will choose. But if you or your company opt out, you will need to find other ways to be competitive and productive. You still need to understand how your colleagues or competitors are operating, and what they are doing well.

Conclusion

Use the list of 12 criteria (and your own, if necessary) to evaluate social media tools and platforms in the workplace. There may be alternative resources that accomplish the same objectives, and in some cases these may even be superior.

In the fast-moving and evolving world of business technology, it is essential to keep evaluating which tools are fit for purpose, and which alternatives could do the job better.

Notes

1 Social media outpaces print newspapers in the U.S. as a news source: www.pewresearch.org/fact-tank/2018/12/10/social-media-outpaces-print-newspapers-in-the-u-s-as-a-news-source (archived at https://perma.cc/W7QQ-9Q9F)

2 11% of Americans don't use the internet. Who are they? www.pewresearch.org/fact-tank/2019/04/22/some-americans-dont-use-the-internet-who-are-they (archived at https://perma.cc/BJT8-UAHD)

3 Internet access – Households and individuals, 2018, www.ons.gov.uk/peoplepopulationandcommunity/householdcharacteristics/homeinternetandsocialmediausage/bulletins/internetaccesshouseholdsand individuals/2018 (archived at https://perma.cc/NF3W-YLZL)

4 MacRae, I and Furnham, A (2017) *Motivation and Performance: A guide to motivating a diverse workforce*, London, Kogan Page

MYTH 2

SOCIAL MEDIA IS FREE

From a practical perspective, the time and complex resources required to effectively manage the many facets of being 'social' make social media activity anything but free.

Introduction

When putting this myth into the mix, we questioned ourselves. Given how widely social media has now been embraced within business, do people really still think of it as 'free'?

One of the key fundamentals of any successful social networking site is a strong user base. Significant volumes of users are necessary to make the concept work – after all, not much socializing or networking happens in an empty room.

The fact of social networks being free has clearly helped to drive increased user numbers. No fees and no barriers to entry makes joining a social network as simple and friction-free as possible, and it's easy for those on the platforms to invite others to join in too.

However, the fact that global mainstream social networks such as Twitter, Facebook, Instagram, LinkedIn, Snapchat and messenger services such as WhatsApp and WeChat (to name just a few) are free to access has historically held back adoption of these communication channels within businesses. Think of the age-old adage: if something is free, people tend not to value it highly. Add to this other challenges and concerns such as data ownership and lack of proprietary platform control, which can make social media channels a risky and unattractive proposition in a commercial setting. The risk is vividly brought to life by this analogy from Scott DeLong, the founder of ViralNova, a start-up business built around Facebook: 'Building a start-up dependent on Facebook is like opening a McDonald's on an active volcano.'[1]

In this chapter we'll explore how the lack of charge for using social networks has potentially impacted the recognition of their significance among businesses, and also how, while the many channels may be fee-free, there are in fact a number of associated costs. From a practical perspective, the time and complex resources required to effectively manage the many facets of being 'social' make social media activity anything but free.

When free isn't really free

There are millions of businesses boasting that Facebook's platform has enabled them to grow and develop in a way that they would not been able to had the platform not existed. Indeed, a 2015 report by Deloitte details how Facebook has stimulated economic growth through three broad effects:[2]

1 as a tool for marketers big and small

2 as a platform for app development

3 as a catalyst for connectivity

The report goes on to state that it estimates that through these three channels, Facebook enabled £176 billion of economic impact and 4.5 million jobs globally in 2014 – excluding the operations of the company itself.

With that sort of impact, and knowing that both start-up businesses and established ones depend on it, it begs the question: if there's real business value in the use of the platform, why does it not charge subscription fees?

One reason may be the competitive landscape. If all social media networks are free, then it sets a precedent for all platforms to fall in line. No one wants to break rank and lose followers to platforms where social is free and easy. However, the main issue is the reality of how these 'forever-free' platforms drive revenue. This brings us back to the size and strength of their user bases, and how this creates the opportunity for businesses and brands to connect with and advertise to relevant audiences.

It's estimated that Twitter generates approximately £2.3 billion per annum from advertising.[3] LinkedIn brings in £1.5 billion annually and Facebook (including Instagram) tops the table at £13 billion.[4,5]

Advertising is big business for the social networks. Their survival depends on those strong user bases, and the millions, or billions, of people sharing their valuable personal data – continuously adding to the digital footprint we each create as we go about our daily lives.

While consumers are becoming increasingly sensitive to their personal data being exploited – a concern that's exacerbated by highly visible data scandals such as the Cambridge Analytica case (in which it was reported that Facebook lost £29 billion overnight) – what this actually means for network advertising revenue is yet to be seen. Currently, there's no evidence of any mass exodus from any of the popular social networking platforms.[6,7]

Beyond targeting social users with adverts, data is also used by brands and organizations to build demographic insights which can be applied to other forms of advertising and product innovation and development. The free use of the social media networks for our data exchange certainly provides more than enough value to keep the networks forever-free.

Insight and management – for a fee

Social listening, as we will discuss in Chapter 6, has become big business. A whole industry has developed around the concept over the last decade, with leading social media monitoring organizations such as Brandwatch and Meltwater delivering real-time digital consumer intelligence, driven by the many conversations, trends and data signals happening across social networks.

Such real-world intelligence enables businesses to better manage and optimize campaign performance, become more effective and agile in their marketing activity, spot opportunities and innovate new products. A recent case study by Danone[8] describes how they listened to relevant comments across social media channels, resulting in the insight that many consumers were seeking lactose-free choices. This resulted in the production of Activia's lactose-free yoghurt.

There are some free ways for businesses to carry out basic social listening, using tools such as Google Alerts, but these are nowhere near as sophisticated or robust as the enterprise-level resources on offer. Of course, such insightful tools come at a cost – with fees starting at a few hundred pounds a month and increasing into the thousands, depending on the functionality and features required.

For businesses active on multiple social networks, there are hundreds of fremium and enterprise-level resources available to help brands and organizations manage their portfolio of accounts. Platforms such as Hootsuite, Sprout Social, Buffer and Salesforce enable all social media accounts to be managed from a central dashboard, making content sharing, scheduling of posts and engagement management far more streamlined – and, in most cases, enable some form of social listening activity too. While some of these platforms have a free offering to get started, the majority are subscription-based – with fees dependent on users and usage, varying from a few pounds to a few thousand pounds per month.

The social media service industry

Social media activity and management is now firmly part of most organizations' digital strategy, and in line with the growing interest in social media engagement from businesses and brands, digital marketing and traditional PR agencies have evolved their offering to include social media services. Specialist social media agencies have also sprung up.

Organizations can make use of these professionals in a number of ways – whether developing social media strategy and campaign development, delivering organic social media management, sharing posts, engaging with customers or managing paid social campaigns. And just as with any agency, the fees vary dependent upon the scale and size of the project in hand. Needless to say, it's highly unlikely that any agency will be working for free!

While it's difficult to determine an estimated value for the social media industry as a whole, Statista suggests:

- revenue in social media advertising segments amounts to £69.8 billion in 2019 – 33 per cent up on 2018
- revenue is expected to show an annual growth rate of 8.7 per cent, resulting in market volume of £97.4 billion by 2023[9]

Advertising is one component of social media revenue; however, as outlined above, so too are there likely to be significant revenues generated by the organizations which have become part of the social media service industry, delivering and supporting related activities including video content development, content development, content marketing, organic social media management, paid social media advertising, social listening, sentiment analysis, channel analytics and data insights – again, to name just a few.

The cost of time

While we've considered the costs of advertising and of outsourcing and procuring solutions relating to social media activity, there are also the very real costs associated with your time. If you're outsourcing the service, it will still take time to manage partners and agencies – and if you're managing internally, there's the time needed to develop and manage internal competence, staffing, and any associated resources such as content development.

According to the We Are Social Digital in 2019 report, the average time spent on social media each day is approximately 136 minutes.[10] If we take the average hourly rate of pay for an employee, and multiply it by those two hours and 16 minutes a day, we can clearly see that there is a wage cost associated with social media activity. That's before we even consider those organizations with dedicated departments, where one or more people are focused on social media activity in a full-time capacity.

Misunderstood at board level

While social media has clearly evolved into a global commercial industry enabling organizations to engage directly with external customers, relevant influencers and even their own employees, organizations still underestimate the reach and influence of social media. The understanding of these channels being 'free', and the misconception that they are largely filled with inane noise and people sharing pictures of their breakfasts (see Chapter 16) has potentially hampered the adoption of social media strategy by organizational leaders.

To this day, there is still confusion surrounding the role of social media within many boardrooms. The belief that the 'social-savvy' apprentice can manage the social media activity for a brand or organization, without any formal marketing and communication training or strategic understanding, has led to a number of social media brand blunders and reputational crises, many of which have been documented in the press, and some of which you can read about in *Great Brand Blunders* by Rob Gray.[11]

If social media channels had never been free to use, and there had always had to be a financial investment into the set-up and procurement of the platforms and implementation expertise from the start (as is the case with global internal communication systems such as CRM or cloud operating systems), then it is highly likely that the social media suite of technologies would have been investigated and better understood far earlier by those making important financial decisions in the boardroom.

This leads us to another arm of the social media industry: education and training, and the associated costs. While we can't find a specific number related to global revenue generated associated with social media training, when searching Google, the term 'social media training' returns a whopping 2,150,000,000 results! A growing number of organizations are making social media training compulsory within their organizations and leadership teams, for example Lego enforcing social media exams.[12]

Training, as with so many other issues associated with social media and mentioned in this chapter, comes at a cost.

Conclusion

From humble beginnings, social media has become a significant and powerful industry, encompassing the development of proprietary and out-of-the-box technical solutions as well as a wide range of service-related solutions including social media management, measurement, training, content development, strategy, consulting, analysis, advertising and training.

While the popular social media platforms have a very clear reason to retain their forever-free positioning, the associated costs of engaging with social media are vast. Using the channels effectively brings a number of very real associated costs. Given the necessary investment into social media activity, it's clear it should be aligned to your business strategy – as getting involved is anything but free.

It's highly likely that social media channels will continue to be free of charge to use, because the data that is generated delivers significant value. As a participant, you are both the customer and the product – your data ultimately drives revenue.

Notes

1   Building a startup on the back of Facebook is like 'opening a McDonald's on an active volcano': www.businessinsider.com/startups-that-rely-on-facebook-2014-1?r=US&IR=T (archived at https://perma.cc/4HLE-6WWF)

2 Facebook's global economic impact: A report for Facebook: www2.deloitte.
com/content/dam/Deloitte/uk/Documents/technology-media-
telecommunications/deloitte-uk-global-economic-impact-of-facebook.pdf
(archived at https://perma.cc/AJB8-2YUC)

3 Twitter ad revenue up 23% to $791 million in Q4 2018: https://martechtoday.
com/twitter-ad-revenue-up-23-to-791-million-in-q4-2018-230530 (archived at
https://perma.cc/GHE9-63TC)

4 A LinkedIn exec explains how the company will hit $2 billion in ad revenue
this year, and why it's betting big on video: www.businessinsider.com/
linkedin-hits-2-billion-in-ad-revenue-bets-on-video-2018-11?r=US&IR=T
(archived at https://perma.cc/TH4R-CZJS)

5 Facebook ad revenue tops $16.6 billion, driven by Instagram, Stories: https://
martechtoday.com/despite-ongoing-criticism-facebook-generates-16-6-billion-
in-ad-revenue-during-q4-up-30-yoy-230261 (archived at https://perma.cc/
T3WK-WUWN)

6 The WIRED guide to your personal data (and who is using it): www.wired.
com/story/wired-guide-personal-data-collection/ (archived at https://perma.
cc/6EGP-KW5U)

7 Facebook lost $37bn overnight due to Cambridge Analytica data scandal:
www.campaignlive.co.uk/article/facebook-lost-37bn-overnight-due-cambridge-
analytica-data-scandal/1459876 (archived at https://perma.cc/F4FL-HYJS)

8 How social listening changed what's in your breakfast bowl: https://corporate.
danone.it/stories/articles-list/social-listening-and-the-rise-of-custom-breakfast.
html (archived at https://perma.cc/CMQ3-HY2A)

9 Social media advertising market statistics: www.statista.com/outlook/220/100/
social-media-advertising/worldwide#market-globalRevenue (archived at
https://perma.cc/WW65-SY4Q)

10 Digital in 2019: https://wearesocial.com/global-digital-report-2019 (archived
at https://perma.cc/4TDF-LVVE)

11 Gray, R (2014) *Great Brand Blunders*, Crimson Publishing, UK

12 Social Brands: Lego forces management to sit social media exams: www.
campaignlive.co.uk/article/social-brands-lego-forces-management-sit-social-
media-exams/1170028?src_site=brandrepublic (archived at https://perma.cc/
F6YR-55MZ)

MYTH 3

ALL SOCIAL NETWORKS DO THE SAME THING

As the channels have evolved, so too has consumer adoption.
The ever-expanding range of features offered has given
business more reasons to get involved with more channels.

Introduction

Communication is a complex beast. What, why and how we communicate differs from person to person, situation to situation, culture to culture, and indeed nation to nation. And not only do cultural and behavioural aspects come into play, but so too does the all-important situational context.

When it comes to who is using social media channels and for what purpose, plenty of continuously updated sources of information provide the latest user statistics. The Social Flagship Report[1] is an excellent, annually updated source of global insight into our social media behaviour, motivation and engagement.

While user demographics and motivations vary from platform to platform, what is clear is that we're at a mass saturation point when it comes to users accessing social media. The report outlines that 98 per cent of digital consumers are social media users, with an average of 8.5 social media accounts, up from 4.8 in 2014. The number of accounts often correlates to the different needs of the user – for example, a person may have their personal profile on Facebook which they use to communicate with friends and family, a Facebook profile for their own personal brand which they use for thought leadership and connecting with clients, influencers and prospects, and then a company profile which is the voice of their organization.

It's clear that the role social media now plays in the lives of its users has significantly evolved. While once upon a time we would have employed social media for more traditional networking, our social media usage has become multifaceted. Given that smartphones have become an extension of our everyday lives, the opportunity for engagement via social media at all times and in any location has enabled the evolution of social platforms into entertainment and commerce platforms.

While social channels may have similar functionality to one another, it's interesting to not only observe your own preferences and behaviour, but also to draw on global research to better understand just how differently we've organically embraced the different channels to serve different purposes.

The fact that people online have an average of 8.5 social media accounts begs the question – why? In this chapter, we'll explore whether all social media channels are the same, taking a closer look at how the most popular channels are being used, and how usage differs from channel to channel.

Twitter

While Facebook and YouTube dominate social media usage, some 326 million people use Twitter every month. This equates to over 500 million tweets being sent each day – approximately 5,787 tweets every second.[2]

Due to the sheer volume of tweets, the crafting of messages tends to adhere to the philosophy 'be brief, be bold, be gone'. The floozy of the social networks, tweets don't stick around for long, as Twitter feeds are constantly refreshing. In fact, when search engine optimization specialists MOZ undertook research to identify the average lifespan of a tweet, they found it to be around just 18 minutes.[3]

While Twitter can be used for communicating, listening, researching, brand building, marketing, initiating connections, networking, and (thanks to the ubiquitous hashtag) reviewing what's 'trending' and finding and joining relevant group conversations, what's really interesting to note is that research by Twopcharts (a site that measures all Twitter activity) identified that almost half of Twitter users never tweet. This confirms the view that the network's users are more interested in gaining information than joining a conversation.[4]

Indeed, if you go to Twitter's home page, you'll see the brand's call to action: 'See what's happening in the world right now' – confirming its position as a real-time news feed.[5] This explains its popularity with sports fans eager to keep up on the latest scores and users looking for gossip, facts, and conversations surrounding key events.

Whether people are following their interests or tuned in to what people are talking about generally, the social network is used as a trusted news source. In fact, most news breaks on Twitter. As a recent example, you only have to follow the #brexit hashtag for all the juicy insight from parliament and political journalists, before it reaches traditional news outlets. And in the US, you can hear directly from the most senior politicians without any filters, editorial guidelines or fact-checking.

Generally, Twitter offers you a simple and quick way to keep your eye on the ball on topics you're interested in. The brevity of the messages means that you can quickly skim through your feed and tune into the general gist of what's happening – as it happens. From a business perspective, this enables you to not only share what's going on in your own firm, but, importantly, to keep up to speed with what's going on in the business landscape, keeping a keen eye on markets, competitors, influencers, customers and potential customers.

LinkedIn

LinkedIn doesn't come close to the mass adoption of Facebook or YouTube, but it still boasts more than 600 million members and over 30 million companies in more than 200 countries and territories.[6] Engagement continues to grow, with professionals signing up to join LinkedIn at a rate of more than two new members per second, and with two million posts, articles and videos published every day.

Individuals use LinkedIn for professional networking, making new connections and job searching. Companies use it for recruiting, business development and sharing company information and brand stories with prospective employees. It's the ultimate online directory of business professionals and organizations, enabling network members to manage their current connections and add new ones to their professional networks.

For organizations, LinkedIn offers an extension of their corporate website, with the ability to share latest news and updates from within the organization. It's useful for both employee engagement and keeping internal team members in the loop, as well as a PR, marketing and business development resource.

The LinkedIn corporate profile is a central hub for connected employees to source and share relevant articles and news – helping to amplify content by sharing it with their networks. It also gives organizations an opportunity to disseminate internal news; new products, services and developments can be shared with a wider audience, both organically and via targeted paid advertising opportunities. A recent blog from Hootsuite found that 94 per cent of business-to-business marketers use LinkedIn to publish content, and 80 per cent of business leads generated via social media come from LinkedIn.[7]

For the individual, having a LinkedIn profile is almost a rite of professional passage. People expect professionals to be available on the platform. Beyond an online CV, it offers the opportunity to create a professional online presence, showcasing personal brand, values, skills, expertise, experience and credibility.

According to a study by the Pew Research Centre, LinkedIn remains especially popular among college graduates and those in high-income households, with 75 per cent of account holders having a university/college degree. And those that use it do so regularly, with 40 per cent of users logging in daily - although the average person spends just 17 minutes per month on the platform.[8,9]

From the various reports highlighted, job-hunting and recruitment, marketing and PR and business networking are most certainly key aspects of why people use LinkedIn. It's a reliable source of professional content too. Via LinkedIn's Pulse news feed, a legion of expert thought leaders, from celebrity CEOs such as Richard Branson and Elon Musk to founders of some of the most successful brands and organizations in the world, regularly share advice and opinions. Indeed, according to LinkedIn's own statistics, 91 per cent of executives rate LinkedIn as their first choice for professionally relevant content.

From the stats, it's clear that LinkedIn is the network most focused on the development of business and professional connections.

Facebook

Facebook is the world's largest social network. Outside China, 85 per cent of internet users say they have a Facebook account, according to the Social Flagship Report.

Although it started as a means for keeping in touch with friends and family and sharing updates, photos and videos, while those aspects still continue to be just as relevant, the platform continues to evolve. Part of its continued appeal stems from its cross-age appeal, which (apart from YouTube) other channels are unable to mirror.

Beyond the Facebook personal profile or company Page, Facebook has a wider functional ecosystem. Facebook Groups enable the development of open and closed communities, and Facebook Messenger, a private and group messaging system, continues to gain traction – offering individuals, brands and organizations a way to liaise in real time.

Within Messenger there are a suite of tools allowing business users to:

- automatically respond to comments on a Facebook post via chatbot
- open up a conversation with a user when they click on an ad
- directly integrate Messenger with an online ecommerce store so that users can immediately view products, make purchases, get receipts, track orders, ask questions and rate the customer experience
- send targeted messages to groups of contacts
- offer a live chat feature on their website
- customize their own chatbot

From a commerce perspective, these innovations provide automated processes that align with consumer channel preference. Given that research from Sprout Social named responsiveness on social media as the number one factor influencing consumers to purchase, Facebook Messenger's features can significantly help in moving buyers along the purchase consideration funnel.[10]

Keeping in touch with friends is also consistently listed as a reason for using Facebook across all age groups. Thanks to Facebook's focus on video and live streaming, the entertainment factor is another key reason users regularly tune in. This trend is most certainly evident with younger demographics, Generation Z (16- to 24-year-olds) and Millennials (25- to 34-year-olds) who, according to the Social Flagship Report, use the platform as an entertainment hub rather than showing interest in other people's status updates.

As well as the networking organic aspects of Facebook, Facebook is fast becoming the largest advertising medium in the world, offering unparalleled granular audience targeting for brands, retail organizations and businesses of all shapes and sizes. The opportunity to direct highly-targeted marketing messages straight to specific audiences is something we'll explore further in Chapter 27.

Facebook advertising most certainly plays a role in influencing individuals, and therefore the purchase journey. The Social Flagship Report states that 42 per cent of people use social media to research new brands or products, making this the second-most important channel overall – and among the 16–24 age group social media comes top, overtaking traditional search engines.

Generally, from a user perspective, Facebook continues to dominate social media engagement for traditional networking, messaging and staying in touch with friends, brands and family, and increasingly via advertising. It's a medium to be influenced by, as well as a way to fill time and be entertained.

WhatsApp

While on the topic of messaging, we can't ignore the influence of WhatsApp as a mobile messenger too. In one of the biggest tech buyouts so far, it was acquired for a whopping £16.9 billion into the Facebook family in 2014, and while Facebook continues to innovate with Messenger features, so too does WhatsApp. As detailed in the Social Flagship Report, while Facebook Messenger has a 5-point lead for the number of users, WhatsApp leads by 5 percentage points in terms of visitor rates, with 1.5 billion users and approximately 60 billion messages sent per day.[11]

If you think about your own usage, it may be that you don't use any social networks to directly connect with others on a regular basis, but you do regularly converse with family, friends and colleagues via WhatsApp.

WhatsApp is unique in several ways, compared to other social networks. Developed to allow users to privately and freely send messages, video and images to each other through their smartphones, it provides a free alternative to SMS (text messaging) which – depending on tariffs – is often still a pay-per-use service. Not only is WhatsApp often more cost-effective than SMS, but it facilitates large group conversations; something that is difficult through SMS, if not impossible.

WhatsApp for Business was launched in January 2018. Positioned as a resource for the small business owner and the mobile app, it enables businesses to interact with customers in just the same way as with the original app.

Generally, WhatsApp is used for group chats – whether that's family, friends, interest groups or teams within organizations.

Snapchat

Snapchat, unlike Instagram and WhatsApp, isn't part of the Facebook group. It remains an independent mobile app messenger service that allows people to express themselves, sharing pictures and videos in the moment that disappear after 10 seconds.

Snapchat were the pioneers of the 24 hour 'story' feature. In the same way that Instagram Stories stick around once saved to Highlights, when saved to Memories, Snapchat content can live on longer than the 24-hour deadline. And while other networks, namely Instagram and increasingly Facebook, have become dominant in this feature, Snapchat currently still has the edge when it comes to augmented reality.

In comparison to Instagram and WhatsApp messenger services, Snapchat comes in a distant third. However, it does see much higher usage figures in North America, particularly amongst 16- to 24-year-olds.

When it comes to business benefits, Snapchat has its uses, particularly when targeting the youth market. For example, Amazon regularly use Snapchat for key promotions such as Black Friday, providing Snapchat-only promotional codes to access deals. This creates a sense of exclusivity for its Snapchat followers.[12]

YouTube

Part of Google, YouTube is currently the largest free video-sharing service in the world, where users can create a profile, upload videos and watch, like and comment on other videos.

Cited as a strong second to Facebook's dominant social platform position, YouTube is perfect for brand building, thought leadership and sharing practical advice. The platform effectively gives individuals, brands and organizations the opportunity to develop their own TV station. And, as with Facebook and Twitter, users can livestream video directly via YouTube.

If we look at visitor numbers per month, YouTube takes the top position. It's the only major social network to have more unregistered visitors than logged-in members. This means that significant numbers of visitors don't bother to log in to their account – or possibly don't even have one. This quirk of user behaviour makes YouTube less a social network and (in the same vein as Google's search engine) more of a social hub – accessible to all, regardless of whether they have an active account.

Heralded as the second largest search engine in the world, Brandwatch reports that 6 out of 10 people prefer watching video on YouTube rather than TV.[13] In fact, 18- to 49-year-olds now spend less time watching TV, while time on YouTube has increased by 74 per cent. On mobile alone, YouTube reaches more 18- to49-year-olds than any other broadcast or cable TV network. On average, there are more than 1,000,000,000 mobile video views per day. These statistics confirm YouTube's firm standing in the entertainment category.

Many individuals have rocketed to superstardom thanks to their broadcasting on the channel. The top 20 most searched channels on YouTube are largely influential 'tubers' who have built significant audiences for their entertaining content, achieving fame – and sometimes fortune.[14]

From a business perspective, the channel is fully embraced as a medium to blend entertainment and commerce. It offers the opportunity to showcase real-world footage, behind-the-scenes insights, product launches, how-to tutorials, expert voices and thought leadership and, of course, entertainment.

Less about networking, YouTube is all about education and entertainment. This aligns with general user motivations for using social media, as cited in the Social Flagship Report: keeping in touch with friends seems to be waning in the 16- to 24-year-old category, dropping 7 percentage points since Q1 2015. It may be that social media as an entertainment hub could potentially outlast social media as a medium for human connection. But based on overall engagement across the platforms, that seems to be a long way off.

Instagram

Part of the Facebook family, Instagram is predominantly a mobile app which offers a fast and simple way to share images and live video with followers.

Instagram has a Stories feature, which allows users to provide behind-the-scenes commentary on what's happening within an organization or brand via images and short video. This is separate to the main feed (often referred to as 'the grid') The feature with the opportunity to share real-world, fly-on-the-wall content is perfect for driving engagement, building audience and sharing product launches, events and of course, promotions. Instagram Stories last for 24 hours, but can be saved to Highlights, adding longevity to real-world events to assist with branding and awareness via the main profile.

Hashtags rule on Instagram, and in many cases are more important than the description text that accompanies the image on the main grid. Up to 30 hashtags can be used on each post to maximize opportunity to connect with relevant conversations, trends and audiences, and up to 10 can be used within each story. From a user perspective, we can search Instagram via hashtags to find new posts or accounts aligned with that hashtag and view which hashtags are trending. The use of hashtags on the platform is fundamental to visibility, growing reach, followers and awareness.

Instagram has over a billion monthly active users, with over 500 million of them using the platform every day.[15] TrackMaven analysed 51 million social media posts from 40,000 different companies over 130 industries to establish which social networks achieve the greatest engagement. The results showed that Instagram dominates when it comes to interactions per follower.[16]

With these high levels of engagement, not only is Instagram visually appealing and simple to scroll through, it has become a powerful platform for brands and marketers looking to connect with a wider audience. It has been shown to influence the buying process, with direct links to promotional landing pages where users can make purchases.

Being a mobile app, Instagram also allows brands and organizations to drive targeted messages, both organically and via paid advertising campaigns, directly into the palms of receptive individuals.

In July 2018, Instagram launched Instagram TV (IGTV), which allows brands, organizations and people to create their own video 'channel' in much the same way as YouTube. Users with standard accounts can upload video content of up to 10 minutes at a time to the channel. For larger brands and creators (aka influencers), there appears to be the scope to upload up to an hour of video per post. Video can either be pre-recorded and uploaded, or recorded live.

This feature represents an opportunity to upload news and updates in a longer format than the usual 15-second video offered within the Story feature or on the main grid. While still relatively new, many brands and businesses are using IGTV to tell a bigger brand story and encourage engagement. For example, BBC News uses it to post compelling headlines and effectively create mini-trailers for their news stories. Each of their IGTV posts includes questions and calls to action, encouraging the viewer to engage in the conversation and share the content with their followers.

Not to be underestimated as just an aesthetically-pleasing news feed, as individuals we're using Instagram to both connect and to promote, to influence and to be influenced.

Changing behaviours and motivations

Social media is integral to product research, with 22 per cent of digital consumers having liked or followed a brand on a social network in the past month. As we've seen in this chapter, regardless of demographics, we tune in to social networks to keep up with the news, interact with our friends and family – and to research new brands or products.

Increasingly, the entertainment offered by social networks plays a key role in motivating us to engage ('filling spare time' ranks as the fourth-most popular reason for using social media according to the Social Flagship Report). This extends to being entertained and engaged by influencers, actors, 'tubers', vloggers and sports and pop stars.

Driving the entertainment factor is our appetite for video content. Live video has become an essential asset, with 28 per cent of users of the four major social platforms outside China engaging with livestreams each month.

Our motivations for using social media have shifted. The emphasis, particularly on some channels, has moved away from networking towards entertainment and shopping. Amidst the shifts, it's clearer to understand why the average user has a range of accounts. While the different channels don't necessarily appeal to different audiences, each one does lend itself to a specific purpose.

Conclusion

Each channel has its own nuances, and collectively they play a significant part in how we connect and communicate. As the channels have evolved, so too has consumer adoption. The ever-expanding range of features offered has given business more reasons to get involved with more channels.

Table 3.1 details user demographics, the percentage of channel adoption across those demographics, and a summary of key function and features.

LinkedIn is still the place for professional connections and recruitment, whiereas Facebook is the traditional networking hub for individuals to keep up to date with friends and family. It's also the place for businesses to share brand story content and build connected communities using Groups, as well as a significant and powerful targeted advertising platform.

Instagram is more aligned with promotion, marketing, brand awareness and increasingly direct shopping. Snapchat, Facebook Messenger and WhatsApp dominate group chat, and while Facebook boasts a stronghold

Table 3.1 Comparing the major social platforms

	Males	Females	Aged 18–29	Aged 30–49	Aged 50–64	Over 64	Function	Other features
Facebook	62%	74%	84%	72%	62%	62%	• Business networking • Staying in touch with friends and family • Targeted paid advertisements or promotion	• Groups • Messenger • Livestreaming • Story function
Instagram	30%	39%	64%	40%	21%	10%	• Promotion • Networking	• Story function • IGTV • Livestreaming
Twitter	23%	24%	40%	27%	19%	8%	• Promotion • Networking	• Lists • Livestreaming
LinkedIn	25%	25%	29%	33%	24%	9%	• Networking • Recruitment • Thought leadership • Targeted paid advertisements or sponsored promotion	• Groups • Livestreaming (as of August 2019) • Blog/publishing article platform
Snapchat	25%	31%	68%	26%	10%	3%	• Promotion • Targeted paid advertisements	• Messenger • Livestreaming • Story function

SOURCE Sprout Social[17]

in the video content arena, YouTube leads the way as the place to go for how-to advice and education (but largely excels at pure entertainment).

Notes

1 Social Flagship Report 2019: www.globalwebindex.com/hubfs/ Downloads/2019%20Q1%20Social%20Flagship%20Report.pdf (archived at https://perma.cc/JZH8-E494)

2 28 twitter statistics all marketers need to know in 2019: https://blog.hootsuite. com/twitter-statistics (archived at https://perma.cc/J9E5-6JKF)

3 When is my tweet's prime of life? (A brief statistical interlude): https://moz. com/blog/when-is-my-tweets-prime-of-life (archived at https://perma.cc/ PB4S-ZPCH)

4 Report: 44% of registered Twitter users have never tweeted: https://mashable. com/2014/04/11/twitter-users-dont-really-tweet/?europe=true (archived at https://perma.cc/X8NR-NNTG)

5 Twitter homepage: www.twitter.com (archived at https://perma.cc/6MA6-E5KC)

6 LinkedIn.com About Us: https://news.linkedin.com/about-us#statistics (archived at https://perma.cc/G4LC-ZGQR)

7 16 LinkedIn statistics that matter to marketers in 2019: https://blog.hootsuite. com/linkedin-statistics-business (archived at https://perma.cc/78VY-VE8D)

8 Social media use in 2018: www.pewinternet.org/2018/03/01/social-media-use-in-2018 (archived at https://perma.cc/GGR8-PD26)

9 46 eye-opening LinkedIn statistics for 2019: https://99firms.com/blog/ linkedin-statistics/#gref (archived at https://perma.cc/LFT2-3KH5)

10 The Q2 2017 Sprout Social Index: https://sproutsocial.com/insights/data/ q2-2017 (archived at https://perma.cc/3QFK-Y8UJ)

11 WhatsApp – The best Facebook purchase ever? www.investopedia.com/ articles/investing/032515/whatsapp-best-facebook-purchase-ever.asp (archived at https://perma.cc/ELV6-M5BG)

12 Brands that are killing it on Snapchat: www.entrepreneur.com/article/286147 (archived at https://perma.cc/9ZTU-MBXS)

13 52 fascinating and incredible YouTube statistics: www.brandwatch.com/blog/ youtube-stats/ (archived at https://perma.cc/6JVH-KQRG)

14 2019's top YouTube searches and channels (so far): www.searchenginejournal. com/2019s-top-youtube-searches-and-channels-so-far/290569 (archived at https://perma.cc/WB28-8JUJ)

15 22+ Instagram stats that marketers can't ignore this year: https://blog.
hootsuite.com/instagram-statistics (archived at https://perma.cc/UV6C-KGU5)

16 The state of social media for business 2016: https://trackmaven.com/blog/
social-media-for-business/ (archived at https://perma.cc/JP4B-6YU7)

17 Social media demographics to drive your brand's online presence:
https://sproutsocial.com/insights/new-social-media-demographics (archived at
https://perma.cc/FF2T-QUTJ)

SOCIAL MEDIA CAN REPLACE YOUR BUSINESS WEBSITE

Businesses will find social media to be most useful when their marketing and other activities revolve around a clear strategy and central platform.

Introduction

Some people run very successful businesses entirely on social media. Indeed, a handful of people and certain organizations operate solely this way – but they are the exception instead of the rule. Social media influencers are examples of successful enterprises operating only on social media, and in some cases only on a single channel, attracting large number of followers with appealing text or image-based content and then promoting products to them. This is nothing new – think of movie stars smoking a certain type of cigarette or drinking a particular drink.

Social media websites are advertising platforms, and provide the opportunity to connect with large numbers of users. They typically operate with a very specific and limited type of content. These platforms and their large audiences can be incredibly useful for businesses – but in most cases are not, and should not be, the only place where a business operates.

Reaching your audiences

Social media is an extremely valuable tool for industry, and is often used for promoting businesses or products (as discussed in Chapters 6 and 16). It can also be used for internal communications (Chapter 13) and for attracting and recruiting employees (Chapter 23), and can supplement a range of other business activities and functions. The potential value of social media to business is difficult to overstate – but it is also necessary to acknowledge some of the limitations.

Social media can be very useful for tapping into the large audiences that already exist on different platforms, and connecting with groups that are already active. Some businesses already use social media as a primary channel for operating – for example, estimates suggest at least half of complaining customers take their concerns to social media.[1] Many customers know that certain companies are so focused on social strategies that the business will be more responsive on their social media than through traditional communication channels.

As with any useful tool, it may be tempting to use only that tool. Social media is typically user-friendly and free to use (however, see Chapter 2 to understand why social media isn't free). This means that barriers to using it are extremely low, with the potential benefits being significant. But social media must be thought of as a supplement to, not a replacement for, the traditional business website and other business tools.

Supplementary, not a replacement

Social platforms are useful for targeting specific audiences for specific purposes. Twitter, for example, is great for time- and location-specific content. Linkedin is more suited to discussions of businesses, workplaces and activities such as recruitment. YouTube provides a platform to share video content with over a billion active users.

Social media companies offer different communications platforms, each with their own unique context, norms and culture (as outlined in Chapter 3). They may offer some level of customization for users, but are generally quite limited in their available features and functionality compared to a traditional business website.

This can be an advantage when business activities on social media are well-designed and integrated into overall business strategy. However, social media can be far less effective when a scattergun approach is used. It may be tempting to create a business page on every social media channel, then just wait to see what happens.

However, businesses will find social media to be most useful when their marketing and other activities revolve around a clear strategy and central platform. This could be anything from their own website to a physical location. As social channels work to expand their own user base, the value of a traditional business website remains as high as ever.

Social media is useful for connecting with potential customers or employees, but many of the most successful businesses use these channels simply to direct people to their products or services on their own site. While the traditional business website may be costly to develop and maintain, it offers far greater customization opportunities.

Some companies do operate primarily on social media, or use it for specific functions. Small businesses can use social media to reduce costs, minimize investment in their own resources and take advantage of the tools on offer. However, it is not a good idea to become over-reliant on social media.

The risks of relying on a third party

While social media can be invaluable, it is important to keep in mind that relying on it can be a risky strategy. Remember that social media companies are not benevolent behemoths. They set non-negotiable terms of use which can, and often do, change substantially.

Social platforms benefit from your customers

Social media companies offer their services for free because of the rewards they get from their users. There are significant advantages for businesses in moving customers or clients away from social media to their own owned channels.

It's easier to think of this using a physical example. If your owned channel is a physical shop where you sell a product, your ultimate goal is to get people through the doors of that shop and buy from you directly. Getting them to that physical location is a necessary first step. It's great if everyone is talking about your shop on social media, but it's not very effective if that traffic doesn't move into the physical space of the shop. If people are talking about your business on Facebook, those are Facebook's customers. They become your customers once you get them into your shop.

It is the same when an owned channel is online. The business's owned space needs to be the focus of any activity on social media. Encourage people to move between channels and through to your owned channel. Social media may be a good shop window, but it needs to get people through the digital door to be effective.

For many businesses, a list of contacts is an extraordinarily valuable resource – these can be business contacts, potential employees, or current and potential customers. Publications, media and resources are also valuable intellectual property, and the online interactions between businesses and their customers can be a goldmine of information. There is significant value in keeping much of this on your own owned channels. This is important for the long-term success and viability of any business, so it is always useful to consider the advantages and disadvantages of publishing your information on social media channels compared with your owned channels.

It's important to remember that the majority of the rewards from your work on social media go to the social media company. For all the interest and online interaction you generate through content, a lot of the benefit goes to that platform. They are more than happy to share their platform with you, so that you can help them obtain user data and advertising revenue. Many businesses and organizations are happy to make this trade-off, but it should be part of a carefully considered strategy.

Social platforms come and go

Some social media consultants live at the mercy of another company's algorithms. They work to generate content that will be picked up by the algorithms of a search engine or social media channel. This is a tactic that may work in the short term, but when the algorithms change, they are left out in the cold.[2]

Social media trends, channels and companies come and go, so businesses must be cautious of depending too much on any particular channel. A business which invests all their time or resources on one social network is putting all their eggs in one basket – and the basket belongs to someone else. The future of that business relies on a single external party.

For a business that has the resources, it can be incredibly useful to invest time and resources in a variety of social channels that fit with its business. This is most effective when the most appropriate channels are used in conjunction with a company's owned channels. Diversification is an important safety and sustainability mechanism for almost all business activity, and it's exactly the same for social media. If your business only had one customer who is 95 years old, it would be seriously advisable to diversify your customer base.

What if your main social media channel were to shut down overnight and all your work was deleted? This happens surprisingly frequently. It may feel unlikely, but it is possible: Vine and Friendster are recent now-defunct social media channels. Tech giant Google alone has had its share of social media sites that have flopped from Orkut, Dodgeball, Jaiku, Wave, Buzz, and more recently, Google+.[3,4]

What happened to the brands or influencers who became popular exclusively on these platforms after they were shut down? If they hadn't built up their owned channels, they would have had to start from square one. Millions of likes, followers or potential customers can disappear just as quickly as they appear.

Conclusion

Owned channels are controlled by your businesses, instead of an external party. This means whoever is creating the content is in control of all aspects of their design, functionality and the data involved. The downside of owned channels is that because they are fully controlled, the required resources and costs also fall on the owner.

In most cases, social media is most effective when it is used in conjunction with owned channels. Businesses and brands can realize all the benefits of a particular social platform's audience and features, and then move people towards their own shop or site.

The lesson is: there is more value and less risk if you can get customers and clients to your business (whether it is a physical or online location). Social media is a great tool for that.

Social media is extremely valuable, and most valuable when it is used strategically. But it is certainly not a substitute for traditional resources like a business website. Each social and owned channel has its own risks, costs and benefits. Analyse each option and consider how to use them in a complementary way.

Be cautious about putting all your eggs in one basket – especially if it is someone else's basket.

Notes

1 The Sprout Social Index, Edition XII: Call-out culture: https://sproutsocial.com/insights/data/q3-2017 (archived at https://perma.cc/2EFH-GVSC)

2 Instagram suddenly chokes off developers as Facebook chases privacy: https://techcrunch.com/2018/04/02/instagram-api-limit (archived at https://perma.cc/BD4H-V9HU)

3 A brief history of Google's social networking flops: http://techland.time.com/2011/07/11/a-brief-history-of-googles-social-networking-flops (archived at https://perma.cc/3APV-VZHK)

4 Google is shutting down its Plus social network sooner than expected after discovering a second security bug: www.cnbc.com/2018/12/10/google-shutting-down-social-network-sooner-because-of-new-security-bug.html (archived at https://perma.cc/D3TU-2H6K)

IT'S NOT POSSIBLE TO MEASURE SOCIAL MEDIA ROI

Each activity on a social channel should have set objectives and a clear purpose. Only once you have identified metrics that really matter can you have any idea whether you are hitting targets

Introduction

There's no doubt about it – social media return on investment (ROI) continues to be a keenly debated topic. A 2018 study undertaken by Sprout Social found that 55 per cent of social media marketers cited measuring ROI as their number one challenge.[1]

So, what's the magic formula for ROI? What should people be measuring when it comes to social media and what returns should they expect to see?

Today, in all realms of digital marketing we've got data coming out of our data, and in recent years there has been an explosion of technologies that enable businesses to track and monitor every move a customer makes – capturing insights and sentiment from the billions of conversations engaged in on social media. Therefore, in this chapter, we'll talk about what organizations need to be considering when they measure ROI, and look at frameworks to ensure this critical component doesn't get missed.

Big Data well and truly exists

According to Gartner, data volume is set to grow 800 per cent over the next five years, estimating 163 zettabytes by 2025). Safe to say, the numbers are mind-blowing, particularly when you consider what a zettabyte looks like (1,000,000,000,000,000,000,000 bytes!).[2]

The tools that provide us with the ability to continuously monitor and measure activity across digital and social media have enabled an equally mind-blowing array of metrics, often to a very granular level. For example, it's not enough to simply understand 'brand sentiment', whether audiences are saying positive or negative things; we can drill further into the context of that sentiment, considering aspects such as 'brand passion' – measuring the level and consistency of a positive feeling.

However, just because we can measure something, it doesn't necessarily mean we get useful or meaningful results. This is particularly true when it comes to measuring ROI.

Measuring ROI is relatively simple for businesses that can tie their social media metrics directly to financial gains. When a direct-to-consumer brand invests £10,000 exclusively in Facebook ads and tracks £30,000 in related online sales, for example, they know the monetary return on their social media efforts.

However, starting with the end in mind is key. We like the not-so-famous quote by US sales trainer and motivational legend, Zig Ziglar: 'Those that aim for nothing hit it with remarkable accuracy.' The sentiment of that quote chimes a highly relevant note when it comes to measuring social media ROI.

In order to gain a true measure of the fundamental return on your investment, you really have to get absolutely clear on what it is you are looking to achieve, as it's that clarity that will help you determine metrics that matter.

With each of the popular social channels, whether Facebook, Instagram, Twitter, Pinterest, LinkedIn, YouTube or Snapchat – it's fair to conclude that they collect, store and publish a lot of data – much of which, is highly visible, and, therefore, pretty simple to measure. Data such as the number of followers, retweets, social shares, comments, likes, loves and other such forms of engagement provide us with some very basic measurement opportunities.

This top-line data, often referred to as 'social signals', offer more of a temperature check as to how content, campaigns and messages are landing with audiences, rather than providing metrics related to overarching objectives aligned with organizational strategy.

For example, if the objective of a campaign is as simple as to grow the baseline of the number of followers a business, brand or account has, then it's very simple to see whether activity moves the dial. While simple, there will be times where such basic metrics are both useful and meaningful; for example, at the outset of any campaign, it's useful to measure whether the number of people following and engaging is expanding or decreasing.

The sheer potential volume of activity, speed and real-time visibility enables teams to pivot and switch tactics if metric markers show that activity is having a negative impact. For example, a leading tech manufacturing organization noticed that during one social advertising campaign, the number of followers across their social media accounts started to quickly decline. It was very apparent that something within the campaign wasn't landing. While the basic metric of the baseline of followers reducing rather than growing didn't tell them specifically why this was the case, it did provide their team with the necessary insights to review the campaign and address any issues, testing aspects that could be responsible for turning their audience off – such as the volume of ads shown, the actual message within the campaign, and the ad timings.

What you measure is contextual

This very basic example shines a light on the larger challenge when it comes to measuring social media activity and social media ROI.

Social technologies are used throughout organizations in different ways. Depending on the focus of the organization, and as discussed further in Chapter 6, social media activity could affect a range of departments; customer service, HR/recruitment teams, PR and marketing, business development and sales and R&D.

Therefore, what you measure and at what point, becomes highly dependent on the context in which social media activity is being carried out, and how it relates to relevant and specific departmental objectives.

For example, for customer service teams, metrics for social media success may focus on speed of response, reduction of escalated incidents or positive sentiment. For marketing, they may look at brand awareness, influencer outreach, lead generation or reputation management. And then of course, there are specific practical campaign aspects such as volume of web traffic, landing page visits, downloads, contact form enquiries, trials, purchases, email list sign ups and so on. There are likely to be numerous data and measurement points to drill into to gain a total understanding of the value that social media activity creates, across the whole organization.

From an ROI perspective, the traditional calculation – resource allocated (time, money, people) deducted from the value created – isn't as clear-cut when it comes to social media activity. The challenge with social media activity is that 'value created' may refer to many things, including the intangible and difficult-to-align-with-directly hard metrics such as revenue generated.

Social media may be supporting and influencing many factors, from brand awareness, new audience engagement, reach of audience, share of voice, website visits, content dissemination and influencer engagement through to more specific value creation such as direct sign-ups, email capture and downloads, as well as direct sales.

Business Insider's Social Commerce Report states that social media is now a major influence on consumer purchasing habits, with 36 per cent of US internet users saying that social networks have become as important as other information sources for making product choices.[3] A similar finding is reported in PWC's Global Consumer Insights Survey, stating that social media channels are the most influential in purchasing decisions.[4] However, measuring direct sales is far easier than measuring influence.

Social media thought leader Gary Vaynerchuck illustrates the challenge of measuring social media ROI with the interesting question, 'What's the ROI of your mother?' Clearly, it's open to significant subjectivity.

However, while we concur that there may not be any one way to measure social, there clearly are some practical ways to measure social media ROI.

Aligning social objectives with organizational goals

The highly-referenced Altimeter Study found that only 34 per cent of organizations feel that their social strategy is connected to business outcomes.[5] To measure value, you need to set social media objectives that are aligned with business and departmental goals.

As highlighted earlier, these objectives may be highly contextual to each campaign or activity, and may change as these progress. When it comes to social media ROI, it's necessary to remain agile, both in terms of what gets measured and when you measure it.

To provide a basic steer, let's take a look at a very simple framework aligning organizational or departmental objectives with specific targets (key performance indicators or KPIs) – providing a baseline to measure success against.

Table 5.1 Organizational objectives with example social KPIs

Organizational/departmental objective	Example social media metric (KPI)
Generate new sales lead opportunities	Deliver 20 trial sign-ups per month
Reduce customer service complaint escalation incidents	Reduce average response time on social to under 45 minutes by end of quarter
Increase awareness of new product prior to launch	Boost mentions and conversational buzz around product launch, creating +10% share of voice by end of quarter

Research from the Trust Radius Social Media Marketing Trend report identified that two of the most challenging aspects of social media programs were measuring social media ROI (60 per cent), and linking social media activities to business outcomes (50 per cent).[6]

It's clear from the basic example framework that in order to link social media activity to business outcomes, it's important to set specific related targets – so that there is clarity on both what you're measuring and how it relates to business objectives. This can be achieved by posing the right questions at the outset:

- What does success look like?
- What objectives/outcomes are we looking to achieve?
- What metrics/evidence do we need so that we can measure progress?
- What discipline will we apply to ensure we are continuously monitoring and learning?

Of course, once you know what it is that you want to achieve and what those metrics/key performance indicators look like, where relevant, you can start to apply a monetary value to them, in order to work out exactly how social media ROI translates commercially.

Dark social – measuring intangible ROI

While we do need to scope specific objectives and the related KPIs for social media activity in order to measure ROI, there is also a healthy dose of intangible value created by social media activity.

The same challenges experienced when measuring other mediums such as PR or advertising campaigns also play out with social media. And just as we can't directly measure the revenue-generating impact of eyeballs on a billboard, so too is it impossible to accurately measure the entire impact of social media attribution.

For example, while we can track granular actions via sophisticated analytics, as well as viewing shares, mentions, comments and other visible forms of engagement, we can't accurately define metrics around those that, for example, read reviews or receive business referrals or product recommendations from friends on a social network, but then visit your business site later via another medium such as a Google search to take action. Referred to as 'dark social' – traffic that can't be tracked – this creates a challenge when it comes to measuring social media ROI.

The other intangible which is difficult to measure is the value of building relationships with audiences on social media. There are many statistics that show the relationship between social media activity, engagement with a brand and purchase loyalty – for example, Big Commerce reports that 30 per cent of consumers would be happy to make a purchase via Facebook, Snapchat or Instagram.[7] Further, 2018 research by GlobalWebIndex found that:

- 40 per cent of social media users are following their favourite brands on social media
- a quarter are following brands on social media from which they might make a purchase
- 2 per cent of consumers say they use social media to research before a purchase[8]

In line with social commerce gaining more traction, ecommerce organizations now measure visitors that come to their sites via social media. MADE. COM, the furniture retailer, identified that visitors to its site from organic social had an average order value 4 per cent higher than the site's average.[9]

Conclusion

It's evident from the statistics and examples in this chapter that measuring social media ROI isn't always clear-cut. There are a number of intangible aspects to consider and complexities across both paid and organic social media activity when it comes to attribution and determining ROI.

Social media has been a movable feast since its inception. The content, strategies and channels which prove effective today may not prove as effective tomorrow, and the same applies for the metrics you choose to measure activity against.

It's necessary to stay close to how social media is performing so that teams and organizations can continuously learn and iterate – and also in order to stay contextual. The message, therefore, is to stay well and truly agile, yet at the same time realistic in how valuable and viable the metrics are. To that end, it's worth sense-checking the following when deciding on metrics:

- Is the metric useful? Does it steer/support decision making?
- Do you have the capacity to measure it effectively?
- Is there a clear reason why you are measuring it?
- Does it align with/feed into your overall business objectives?

Each activity on a social channel should have set objectives and a clear purpose. Only once you have identified metrics that really matter – and have set off with the end in mind – can you have any idea whether you are hitting targets. (Remember that quote from Zig Ziglar!)

Clarify your objectives by asking:

- What does success look like? What objectives/outcomes are we looking to achieve?
- What evidence do we need to measure progress?
- What discipline will we apply to ensure we are continuously monitoring and learning?

In the world of social media, finding ROI is indeed possible – but only if you have set out with very clear objectives and KPIs. Therefore, before you dive in, start with the end in mind.

Notes

1   How to define an actionable social media ROI for your business: https://sproutsocial.com/insights/social-media-roi (archived at https://perma.cc/6GUF-NHL6)
2   Just how big is Big Data: https://waterfordtechnologies.com/just-big-big-data (archived at https://perma.cc/2L2J-7D62)
3   The Social Commerce Report: www.businessinsider.com/business-insider-social-commerce-report-2019-7 (archived at https://perma.cc/444S-D3M7)
4   Global Consumer Insights Survey 2018: www.pwc.com/gx/en/retail-consumer/assets/consumer-trust-global-consumer-insights-survey.pdf (archived at https://perma.cc/Y9SW-L5TN)

5 New research: The ROI of social media management tools: www.prophet.com/2017/08/roi-of-social-media-management-tools (archived at https://perma.cc/D7JH-2NGT)

6 2015 Social Media Marketing Trends Report: www.trustradius.com/buyer-blog/2015-social-media-marketing-trends-report (archived at https://perma.cc/85L4-3JVH)

7 The secret to the future growth of your ecommerce channel: Social commerce: www.bigcommerce.co.uk/blog/social-commerce (archived at https://perma.cc/EJX5-BQRN)

8 Social media is increasing brand engagement and sales: www.forbes.com/sites/tjmccue/2018/06/26/social-media-is-increasing-brand-engagement-and-sales (archived at https://perma.cc/6Q9X-LJTW)

9 MADE.COM on the value of social commerce: https://econsultancy.com/made-com-on-the-value-of-social-commerce (archived at https://perma.cc/RV63-5GTH)

MYTH 6

SOCIAL MEDIA ACTIVITY IS PURELY A MARKETING FUNCTION

Social media activity is a two-way, one-to-many and many-to-many communication resource, and presents a rich pot of insight from which numerous business units can draw.

Introduction

From their introduction almost two decades ago, social networks have grown from niche communication tools for early adopters into hyper-targeted, multi-media resources used by billions of people every day, worldwide.

Heralded from the outset in the business community as a new and potentially far-reaching channel to market, it was no surprise that social media was initially always managed within marketing departments. Social media directors, managers, executives, consultants and gurus didn't exist. Neither did social media agencies, and there was no such thing as a 'social media strategy' or targeted advertising directly to highly-relevant social audiences.

Over the same timeframe, digital technology has continued to advance at a blistering rate and due in large part to the ferocious adoption of the smartphone and associated mobile technology, social media is widely and easily accessible.

Depending on the size and structure of an organization, it's still not unusual for social media management to sit somewhere within the marketing division. There's a natural fit with the very essence of marketing: brand awareness, customer acquisition, customer loyalty, promotions, creative content and audience engagement – both organically and via paid advertising and sponsorship.

However, as we will also touch on in Chapter 10, far from swimming in its own lane, social media and its variety of applications is widely relevant for many organizational departments. It is, or should be, enmeshed within customer service, HR, PR, product development, IT, legal, R&D, sales, business development, PR and corporate communications.

In this chapter, we'll look at how social media makes an impact outside the marketing sphere. We'll focus on external-facing and then internal-facing social media activity, and look at where they both fit.

External-facing social activity

Customer service

As always-connected consumers, our customer service expectations have risen in line with technological advances. We expect to be able to contact a business at pretty much any time of day, via our channel of preference – and, importantly, we expect a speedy response.

No longer an optional extra, social media and customer service are now completely synonymous. If things are not going our way; whether it's the fact that our train is delayed, the service we receive is poor or even just slow – or our expectations are dashed by shoddy quality or misrepresentation, then hell hath no fury like our fast fingers on a smartphone keypad.

And of course, social media is not purely used for complaining. When it comes to customer service, we are using social media to ask questions and receive answers and advice.

Research on customer service usage of social networks identified that:[1]

- 1 in 3 social media users prefer social media customer care services to telephone or email;
- an estimated 67 per cent of consumers now use social media networks to seek resolution for issues;

- customers spend 20–40 per cent more with companies that engage and respond to customers via social media;
- nearly 70 per cent of consumers have said that they have used social media for issues to do with customer service on at least one occasion.

The customer service team is often the first point of contact for a brand or organization – often relevant across the entire customer journey – before, during and post-purchase. This level of real-time, highly responsive connectivity is of course all part of brand marketing – yet owned and managed directly by the same customer service team advising and responding.

There are many case studies now showing effective use of social media for customer service. The article 'Social customer service: Lessons from 5 of our favourite brands' includes case studies from Nike, Spotify, Skyscanner, Netflix and Starbucks.[2]

It's an increasing strategic resource, and customer service teams are embracing the latest technologies evolving from the social platforms, taking advantage of artificial intelligence to segment and speed up customer response times and recognizing that there are a lot of customers that don't simply want to vent on social media, but rather want a private conversation, without losing responsiveness. Thus, many customer service conversations are moving into messenger services such as Facebook Messenger.

One such example is Great Western Railway in the UK, who are championing Messenger as their primary channel in their social strategy – committing to 90 per cent real-time issue resolution.[3] As social channels continue to evolve to enable organizations to service queries faster and in a more targeted way, this chimes well with the need to meet targets and customer service objectives.

Human resources

A company wanting to be found by a large pool of talented candidates, or wanting access to that same pool of individuals, cannot ignore social media. For HR teams, social media focused platforms such as LinkedIn have become a staple tool.

Social media gives HR teams the opportunity to reach a far larger number of prospective employees at relatively low cost on a continuous basis. For example, HR teams can communicate organizational culture – showcasing the employer brand, sharing stories and case studies from happy employees, leaders and managers and giving an overview of workplace features and benefits, in order to entice the right prospective employees.

There's also the opportunity for HR teams to set up employee referral schemes, which leverage the contacts their staff have in their personal networks. Employee referrals have the highest applicant-to-hire conversion rate, accounting for 40 per cent of all hires.[4] Clearly, a strong talent acquisition tactic will encourage employees to share hiring opportunities with their networks. Social media can help HR teams mitigate the costs and brand reputation associated with making the wrong hire.

According to a 2018 Career Builder Survey, 70 per cent of employers use social media to screen candidates during the hiring process.[5] That's a relatively high percentage of employers relying on the collective use of social media to inform their decisions. However, a 2019 *Raconteur* article suggests that using social media as a screening tool may provide more details than a company needs – which may lead to bias and ultimately hamper diversity in the workforce.[6] Conversely in the same article, Manpower Group claim that social media opens up the talent pool to a far more diverse group of candidates.

Research and development

When it comes to social media, market research isn't always considered a key use. However, given that more than three billion people around the world are active on social media for an average of two to three hours a day, and the fact that they tend to share a lot of information about themselves online, there is a significant pot of data from which to collect rich insights.

For example, when GE Life Sciences wanted to learn how customers discussed protein purification, they analysed 500,000 protein-related comments on social media. The data improved their content creation, enabling them to tailor their website in a way which was more aligned with the voice of the customer, and optimize their search strategy.[7]

Referred to by Curt Bloom, then-President of Crimson Hexagon, as 'the biggest focus group on the planet', social media can also assist with getting direct feedback about products, services, new features and beta tests – enabling brands and organizations to optimize in line with the wisdom of the crowd.

Whether it's polls, social listening or interpreting reams of data to analyse audience sentiment, social media has become an important resource in the field of research and development.

Sales

Networking has always played a valuable role for business development and sales professionals. Social networks have become equally valuable, enabling a far wider array of connections and the ability to tune in to what's happening on the ground with prospects and customers.

'Social selling' is the process of sales professionals using social media to find and engage with new prospects. It's effectively the same practice of building rapport and relationships with your prospects in real life – so that when they are ready to buy, you will be top of their mind.

With social technologies, sales professionals are able to share relevant content, answer questions, respond and continuously engage from the very start of the purchase funnel all the way through to consideration, building rapport and closing the deal.

Taking the time to engage with social selling reaps rewards. Salesforce reports that 78 per cent of social sellers outsell peers who don't use social media, and 39 per cent of business-to-business professionals said that they were able to reduce account and contact research time using social media.[8]

Internal-facing social activity

In the same way as external-facing social media activity provides opportunities to listen to audiences, engage and connect with customers, prospects and influencers, share marketing messages and keep audiences up to speed with company notices and PR, all these highly valuable activities can be harnessed and used for internal audiences.

Research shows that 82 per cent of employees believe that social media improves work relationships, and 60 per cent believe social media supports decision-making processes.[9] It has the potential to ease collaboration, make employees feel more involved and connected to their employers, and aid retention.

Customer service

As mentioned, it's common for the customer service team to have a front-line presence on social media, managing day-to-day conversations and queries with the customer. Such engagement will drive useful insights, which the customer service team can feed back into the business to help drive continuous improvement.

HR

According to the Career Builder Survey mentioned earlier, around 43 per cent of employers use social media to check on current employees. After talent acquisition, once organizations have invested in the right people, it's a case of nurturing them and engaging with them in a way that ensures continued productivity.

There are some frightening statistics about the level of employee disengagement – with Gallup's 2018 State of the Global Workplace Report suggesting that a whopping 85 per cent of employees are either unengaged or actively disengaged at work. The economic consequences of this are approximately £5.4 trillion in lost productivity.[10]

A growing number of case studies demonstrate the positive impact of social media being used internally to regenerate employee engagement. We'll outline these in more detail in Chapter 13.

Communications/internal marketing

Social media offers the same benefits for communication and internal marketing teams to effectively connect and engage with internal customers as it does for external-facing teams to connect with customers. Businesses increasingly recognize that keeping their workforce (that is, their internal customers) happy and engaged is just as important as keeping external customers happy; it is fundamental to productivity and business performance.

EY report that using social media for internal communications opens new channels for innovation, dialogue and insight, and integrates employees into the company culture; a major driver of employee engagement.[11]

To really show the connection between engagement and productivity, a study by McKinsey Global Institute discovered that if companies were to fully implement social media activity internally, they could improve employee productivity by 20 to 25 per cent.[12]

Strategy/leadership

Many of the research articles that we've mentioned describe the role that leaders play in driving organizational connectivity, by staying visible and communicating effectively with employees.

A growing swathe of CEOs are taking to the external-facing social media stage – speaking out to keep investors, the media and customers aware of important company updates or viewpoints. However, from an internal perspective, social media technologies enable all leaders, at every level within an organization, to connect and communicate openly and directly with the teams they lead.

Communication is not a one-way street, either ; social media channels offer the opportunity for leaders to listen directly to what employees are saying and, where relevant and appropriate, to respond directly.

Employee advocacy programs achieve the most success when they have leadership buy-in. Not only is getting leadership involved good for business, but there's opportunity to build the all-important trust. 2016 research from Brandfog found that 75 per cent of respondents felt a leader being active on social media made them more trustworthy.[13]

Conclusion

Social media activity is a two-way, one-to-many and many-to-many communication resource and presents a rich pot of insight from which numerous business units can draw. This naturally leads to questions over how social media should be managed, via a central division that services each aspect of the business or with each business unit managing their own activity.

Coming back to the myth of whether social media is purely a marketing function; as we've seen throughout this chapter, it's clear that social media activity transcends the confines of any one department.

Notes

1 Social media customer service statistics and trends: www.socialmediatoday.com/social-business/social-media-customer-service-statistics-and-trends-infographic (archived at https://perma.cc/E5CZ-KBXK)

2 Social customer service: Lessons from 5 of our favourite brands: https://mention.com/blog/social-customer-service (archived at https://perma.cc/CTX7-GZRA)

3 Case study: How Great Western Railway uses Messenger for social support: www.conversocial.com/case-studies/gwr (archived at https://perma.cc/NN7J-6A9T)

4 Why employee referrals are the best source of hire: https://theundercoverrecruiter.com/infographic-employee-referrals-hire (archived at https://perma.cc/B2TH-PF5C)

5 Keep it clean: Social media screenings gain in popularity: www. businessnewsdaily.com/2377-social-media-hiring.html (archived at https:// perma.cc/R9W4-UAH4)

6 Is social media strengthening our biases: www.raconteur.net/hr/social-media-biases (archived at https://perma.cc/MT3K-54D9)

7 How to use social media for market research: https://conversionxl.com/blog/ social-media-market-research (archived at https://perma.cc/6XLS-VT8K)

8 What is social selling and how does it work? www.salesforce.com/ blog/2017/08/guide-to-social-selling.html (archived at https://perma.cc/3K7P-S39C)

9 Employees who use social media for work are more engaged – but also more likely to leave their jobs: https://hbr.org/2018/05/employees-who-use-social-media-for-work-are-more-engaged-but-also-more-likely-to-leave-their-jobs (archived at https://perma.cc/6X5T-EMBX)

10 State of the global workforce report: www.gallup.com/workplace (archived at https://perma.cc/V5GD-RPSP)

11 Using social media to engage your workforce: https://consulting.ey.com/ using-social-media-to-engage-your-workforce (archived at https://perma. cc/6P4A-J9RF)

12 5 reasons social media in the workplace can help employees: https:// theolsongroup.com/5-reasons-social-media-workplace-can-help-employees (archived at https://perma.cc/TX8U-UUEX)

13 Survey CEOs social media and brand reputation: http://brandfog.com/ BRANDfog2016CEOSocialMediaSurvey.pdf (archived at https://perma.cc/ UAK4-9H7D)

SOCIAL MEDIA MARKETING IS A DARK ART

Social media can be used to sell everything from useless products to toxic ideologies. But just because technology can be used unethically, it does not mean that the entire technology is evil. It just means that efforts must be made to use it in an ethical way.

Introduction

Is social media a force for good or evil? There's no clear-cut answer, as social media has clearly been used for both positive and negative purposes. Much of the early discussion about social media talked about it being a positive force. Facebook founder Mark Zuckerberg said in 2012: 'By giving people the power to share, we're making the world more transparent'. The following year, Twitter founder Jack Dorsey said: 'When people come to Twitter and they want to express something in the world, the technology fades away. It's them writing a simple message and them knowing that people are going to see it.'

Like any technology, as social media platforms have grown from niche to mass adoption, there are both evangelists and critics. And the following interesting recent example shows, there certainly can be a dark side to social media.

Social media can be manipulated

The Americans have the strongest conventional military on earth, but the Russians seem to be ahead of their time in meme warfare.

Russia's Internet Research Agency (IRA) has been causing headaches for a long time, and their malicious activities were an open secret. An exposé in the *New York Times* in 2015 said that 'From a nondescript office building in St Petersburg, Russia, an army of well-paid "trolls" has tried to wreak havoc all around the Internet – and in real-life American communities.'[1]

Their online activities can be directly traced back to 2011, when what may have started as pro-Kremlin operations inside Russia expanded worldwide with remarkable speed.

On 11 September 2014, an elaborate and well-organized social media hoax spread panic about a supposed terrorist attack on a chemical plant in Louisiana. Hundreds of Twitter accounts were spreading false news and videos of a chemical plant exploding, including supposed local footage. Journalists, politicians and local influencers were bombarded with news of this supposed attack, with links to other social media sites including video footage on YouTube, doctored photos suggesting the story had been picked up by CNN, and screenshots purporting to be alerts from the chemical plant.

This hoax followed a similar pattern to other attacks that occurred around the US in 2014, for example, a well-organized social media campaign suggesting Ebola had spread to Atlanta. Again, this involved campaigns of social media posting, targeting media, influencers and politicians, links to other social media, and even fake websites that appeared to be identical to the websites of local news outlets and government bodies, but which included the fake stories about attacks.

The investigation by the *New York Times* found that the Moscow-based IRA were spreading stories, faking comments and attempting to influence news and shape opinions around the world. Much of the activity focused on influencing opinion related to the civil war in Ukraine and churning out comments and content that were positive about the Kremlin. A great deal of negativity about Barack Obama also featured. The IRA had strict performance targets, and were focused on metrics such as page views, comments, likes and other online data. Employees would work 12-hour days and would have to meet quotas such as five political posts, ten non-political posts and up to 200 comments per day. In other words, the IRA had an ambitious and grueling objective to shape online opinion both inside Russia and outside it. The employees were paid well for their time: in 2014, the salary was 41,000 rubles per month (around £500), but by 2016 this had risen to £1,083 per week.[2]

It may seem like an expensive organization to run, but recent research shows it has had widespread effects on social media, and for a national government, estimates suggests its running costs for a year are cheaper than a single cruise missile.[3]

While there was initial speculation about Russia's influence, there is now hard evidence that the IRA spread their own information, memes and fake news related to the US Presidential election in 2016. Oxford University's Computational Propaganda Research Project conducted a comprehensive study, commissioned by the US Congress, of the IRA's influence.[4]

The IRA used fairly standard tactics to spread information on major social media networks like Facebook, Twitter and Instagram. They reached tens of millions of users in the US, and over 30 million users shared content from IRA-controlled pages. The IRA ran dozens of pages, targeting different demographic and interest groups representing diverse communities from across the US.

They specifically used different types of pages to target different groups, with group names like 'Being Patriotic' (over 6 million likes), 'Heart of Texas' (over 5 million), 'Blacktivist' (more than 4.5 million), 'United Muslims of America' (about 2.5 million), 'LGBT United' (about 2 million) and 'Brown Power' (about 2 million). The research from Oxford showed that they targeted right-leaning groups with pro-Trump advertising, while spreading information to minority and left-leaning groups designed to spread mistrust in institutions, all the time encouraging people not to vote.

As has long been the practice by the IRA, the majority of the content was not political, but intended to encourage engagement and collect more followers using clickbait, humour and memes. One of the interesting observations about the IRA's tactics is that they are similar in many ways to commercial practices that aim to gain influence on social media and in marketing.

It is not uncommon to create a range of groups across different platforms to promote a product or a brand. Targeting certain interest groups is certainly a typical marketing practice (see Chapters 16 and 28). That's not to say that what they did was good or right, but these are not hackers – they are a large, well-organized and knowledgeable organizations taking advantage of the infrastructure that is already available.

The IRA built on many of the social media marketing tactics that were already in widespread use. They drew on fairly legitimate practices that would have been familiar with the marketing textbooks – microtargeting, customer segmentation, uses of multimedia in spreading messages – and they were certainly adept at using memes.

While the ultimate goal was subversive, many of the tactics used were within the normal and legal range of internet activity.

Lessons for social media marketers

Marketing has long been accused of being a type of 'dark art'. Attempting to influence people to buy products, sway opinions and encourage specific behaviours has the potential to draw criticism.

Advertising campaigns about smoking are a prime example: early slick advertisements attempted, quite successfully, to portray inhaling a cocktail of carcinogens as fun, youthful, sexy and healthy. Lucky Strikes were marketed as 'Your throat protection against irritation, against cough' or 'More doctors smoke Camels than any other cigarette' – even 'As your dentist, I would recommend Viceroys' (a brand of cigarettes).

Many of the tactics used by the IRA are fairly basic techniques for spreading messages used by many marketing organizations:

- **Create memorable, shareable content** – create content, whether articles, lists, photos, videos or memes, that makes a strong and immediate impression. Content should be on topics that people want to discuss on social media and share with their friends or connections.

- **Create topical content** – content that is current and relevant will generate more user engagement, garner interest and draw people into the discussion.

- **Repurpose popular content** – revise and reuse the most popular content in different ways or on different channels. Repackage and revise 'evergreen' content in diverse ways for diverse audiences.

- **Engage your audience** – get activity and posts that encourages people to like, comment and share. This will attract a larger audiences – social media sites will promote and feature content that is generating a great deal of interest.

- **Work with influencers** – collaborating with popular users or channels can get people interested in those connections, the relationships between different influencers and their content.

Social media can be used to sell everything from useless products to toxic ideologies. But just because technology can be used unethically or with malicious intent, it does not mean that the entire technology is evil. It just means that efforts must be made to use it in an ethical way.

We've used the example of Russia's IRA not to scare individuals or companies away from social media, or to convince anyone that social media is inherently dark or negative. We've used them because it's not an organization trying to build a positive international reputation. Nor is it attempting to attract customers or foster good feelings. The contrast is a useful one, because it's an example of an organization that does not seem particularly concerned with getting negative press in countries outside of Russia.

Companies, organizations and individuals who want to build a positive reputation or interact with groups and communities and individuals on social media should not use dark or destructive methods to achieve their aims. The lesson here is that eventually the truth will be found out. This type of unethical activity would be incredibly damaging for any company operating in a democratic country.

Those using social media should make sure their activities adhere to strong, ethical guidelines.

Ethical guidelines: a defence against the dark arts

To ensure you're not being seen as practicing dark arts, we've included ethical guidelines for activities on social media adapted from National Social Marketing Centre guidelines:[5]

- **Avoiding discrimination against certain groups**: do not deliberately exclude certain groups, and avoid using harmful stereotypes or prejudice against these groups.

- **Minimizing potential harm**: be careful when attempting to influence people's beliefs or call them to action. A common example of this on social media is threats or incitements of violence. This type of activity is not just unethical; it is also often illegal.

- **Informed and voluntary consent**: be clear and transparent about what activities you are carrying out, how any data the company collects will be used, and the effects of any user interaction. The General Data Protection Regulations (GDPR) in the EU comprehensively covers your responsibilities.

- **Respect for privacy and confidentiality**: this is closely tied to informed and voluntary consent. People who engage with an organization's social media must be clearly informed what data they are sharing and how it will be used. When organizations engage in activities such as handling complaints or using customer feedback on social media, privacy and confidentiality must be respected.

- **Honesty and avoiding deception**: any organization using social media as part of their business should be direct and honest about what their activities are and why they are doing it, and should not use social media to lie or misinform. When mistakes happen, there should be a mechanism to clarify or correct.

- **Avoiding (or declaring) conflicts of interest**: this is particularly relevant for marketing content. Influencer accounts often contain a mix of general content and paid content from third parties. Declaring conflicts of interest is simple: be clear and honest about any third parties who have a relationship with the content.

These guidelines can serve as a useful template, but any company with a social media strategy should develop their own policy for social media use. There may be different requirements for different business activities, and most professional associations will have their own advice that must be integrated.

The National Social Marketing Centre provides a useful outline, along with a detailed handbook on developing your own ethical guidelines.

Conclusion

Social media can be used for good or ill, and can be full of good and bad actors. There will be people who use any sort of technology with ill intentions. That is not to say the technology is necessarily bad. When companies, organizations and influencers use social media, they should abide by a clear set of ethical standards. Laws, regulations and professional guidelines are a useful place to start.

However, it's worth noting that technology adapts and changes much faster than any regulations or professional standards – so it's important constantly to revisit your ethical advice. Those using social media should make sure their guidelines for social media reflect the company's vision, strategy and own ethics.

Notes

1 The Agency: www.nytimes.com/2015/06/07/magazine/the-agency.html (archived at https://perma.cc/9946-P4CE)

2 Inside the Russian troll factory: Zombies and a breakneck pace: www.nytimes.com/2018/02/18/world/europe/russia-troll-factory.html (archived at https://perma.cc/6C94-UZ8J)

3 Exclusive: Putin's 'chef,' the man behind the troll factory: https://edition.cnn.com/2017/10/17/politics/russian-oligarch-putin-chef-troll-factory/index.html (archived at https://perma.cc/E5FB-AYG9)

4 The IRA, social media and political polarization in the United States, 2012–2018: https://comprop.oii.ox.ac.uk/wp-content/uploads/sites/93/2018/12/The-IRA-Social-Media-and-Political-Polarization.pdf (archived at https://perma.cc/V58M-GUJR)

5 Social media ethics: http://eprints.uwe.ac.uk/54/1/NSMC_Ethics_Report.pdf (archived at https://perma.cc/CZ9M-KBCC)

SHARING MORE CONTENT IS ALWAYS BETTER

The brief and limited format of social media platforms can actually help to sharpen your techniques and clarify your messaging. It can force you to be succinct and pithy.

Introduction

If you look for guidelines for posting on social media, you will find all sorts of suggestions and recommendations: how much to share, how often, what times of day and what sort of images, video, infographics and other media that can be useful to get your message across. These can be very helpful, but remember, these are guidelines – not absolute rules.

Generally, Monday through to Friday during regular working hours are the most active times on social media. Friday and Saturday evenings often have lower activity, and the fewest people are online in the middle of the night (about 10 pm to 4 am). But if your business promotes something related to nightlife, Friday and Saturday evenings might be better. If you are selling hangover cures, Saturday and Sunday mornings might be the best times to advertise your products. If you're advertising online casinos, perhaps 10 pm to 4 am are peak times for your customers.

While oversharing or over-saturating users with content is not ideal, being inactive is just as bad. Any business that started a social media profile a decade ago, posted a few dozen times in that period and has been inactive for the past few years should be embarrassed. It's better not to have a social media profile than to have one that is clearly neglected and ignored.

Let's start with oversharing. Oversharing can either mean posting too frequently, or sharing details that are far more personal than strangers on the internet want to hear. It can be a minor inconvenience to readers, but some people take it to the level of a digital plague, splurging so much incomprehensible or unnecessary information that it blots out the sun for days.

Getting too personal

Oversharers are great from the perspective of a hiring manager. If someone puts all the details of their lives and a history of their own behaviour and social interactions with others online for all to see, that information may be seen as fair game when it comes to making hiring decisions.

If someone has a long history of being openly and publicly belligerent, of initiating and fuelling arguments and being consistently aggressive (or passive-aggressive) towards friends and/or strangers, that may be a good indication of their likely future behaviour in the workplace. If people display serious problems with judgement and impulse control on social media, a hiring manager may justifiably decide that their actions would not be desirable in the office.

We discuss what kind of information is fair game in Chapters 22, 23 and 24, but the rule of thumb is that if someone makes their own information publicly available, other people are likely to see it. Whether or not employers are allowed to access this information and consequently make employment decisions based on it is another matter, depending on the country, local employment and data protection regulations, as well as the nature of the work.[1,2]

Social media can be a double-edged sword. According to a Harris Poll, 54 per cent of recruiters say they have decided not to hire a job candidate because of information they saw on the candidate's social media profiles.[3] However, too little can be just as bad as not enough. Over half (57 per cent) also said they are less likely to interview a candidate who they could not find online, and 44 per cent said they found information on social media that made the candidate a more desirable hire.

When people choose to share their own personal information, the outcomes are their responsibility. But what about when people decide to overshare a company's or customer's information? That way leads to danger.

Loose lips sink ships

How often do employees share private or confidential company information on social media? All the time. It's worse than a bit of office gossip or loose lips at the pub, because once it's posted on social media, it's very difficult or impossible to delete. There was an instructive and amusing case in 2013, when struggling UK music retailer HMV went through a large process of layoffs. Thanks to Twitter and screenshots, the social media saga of a disgruntled employee live-tweeting the entire process is still visible to this day.[4]

The tweets began at about 9 am, describing the layoffs process in lurid detail from the inside: 'We're tweeting live from HR where we're all being fired! Exciting!!' They went on: 'Under usual circumstances, we'd never dare to do such a thing as this. However, when the company you dearly love is being ruined…'

The very public and very trending tweets went on to detail how angry the people being fired were, as well as going into detail about the process and those involved. 'Just overheard our Marketing Director (he's staying folks) ask "How do I shut down Twitter?"'

The tweets continued on and off throughout the day, with various details emerging, apparently in a struggle for control over the corporate Twitter account between those employees remaining with the company and those being laid off. Most of the posts were deleted from Twitter, but the records will remain on the internet, with the final tweet of the saga reading: 'There have been job losses today, but not in our stores. We are still open for business, thx for your continued support #savehmv'. Save HMV, indeed. Not great PR for an already-floundering business.

It is easy to make mistakes, though, and sometimes smart and well-meaning people make gaffes on social media. In 2014 Twitter's CFO accidentally published some very sensitive details about a company acquisition publicly instead of in a private message: 'I still think we should buy them. He is on your schedule for Dec 15 or 16 – we will need to sell him.'[5]

Although these kinds of mistakes are easy to make, they can have significant consequences.

This is why it is important to have a sensible policy and clear practice guidelines for social media use in the workplace. The EU General Data Protection Regulation (GDPR) makes this even more important, laying out company responsibilities for recording, accessing and secure storage and access of data. We'll discuss this in greater detail in Chapter 24.

The General Data Protection Regulation (GDPR)

In Europe, all companies are required to meet certain regulatory requirements if they process and handle data. This means there are fairly strict rules, and if a company or employee shares someone's personal data or information on social media, the company would fall foul of the data protection regulation. Here are some quick facts about GDPR:

- Any data about individuals held by a business (including customers and employees) is considered 'personal data'.

- Companies are responsible for any breaches or problems affecting that data. This includes if it is lost or damaged, hacked, stolen or otherwise compromised (including being shared without consent on social media).

- Generally, people must consent to having their data collected, and be informed about how it will be used.

- Anyone is allowed to access the data that a company stores about them. This includes what type of data, the exact data, where it has been used and who it has been shared with. Any sharing or posting of someone's personal data on social media will raise some awkward questions (as well as being a legal violation).

- In the case of breaches of GDPR, companies can be fined of up to €10 million or 2 per cent of the firm's global turnover (whichever is the greater).

- Within the first year of GDPR, there were 20,000 complaints made and €56 million in fines issued across Europe (although Google accounts for more than 90 per cent of those fines).[6]

Brands oversharing

Companies also can overshare on social media. It's great to be active, to connect directly with customers and be responsive on social media. But it's best not to bog people down with an incessant stream of fatuous content. Or course this isn't restricted to social media – some companies have always bombarded consumers with endless trivial and saccharine content.

It's important that companies be educated and savvy consumers and users of social media, and avoid taking some of the bad habits of the past online. If you want to saturate people with low-cost and high-frequency content, social media will certainly support that. But it is not the best way to get people's attention or admiration for your brand.

The brief and limited format of social media platforms can actually help to sharpen your techniques and clarify your messaging. It can force you to be succinct and pithy. Keep in mind that if you need a to spread your message across 14 successive tweets connected with ellipses, perhaps the message needs some refining (either that, or you need a different platform).

Post-happy social media managers

Let's quickly mention some of the problems that can occur when social media managers are careless and too quick to post. Then we'll discuss how much is too much to share:

- **Sharing from the wrong account**. Many people, especially those who manage social media accounts for themselves, their company, and for other organizations or projects have multiple social media accounts (sometimes for completely different purposes). Maybe a company's social media manager volunteers their skills to manage the social profiles of a charity. Perhaps they have their own personal page, pages for their pets, projects or political views. Then, if they are a bit too quick to post, they end up posting the wrong thing to the wrong account. Easy to do – but the consequences can vary from minor to severe.

- **Mixing up direct messages and public posts**. This happens all the time too, like the example from the CFO of Twitter accidentally hinting at a company acquisition in a public post instead of a direct message. It's a very easy mistake to make, so it is necessary to make sure company social media accounts are clearly separated from other accounts.

- **Sharing your search queries**. Ever post something on social media that you meant to search for? Instead of typing it in to the search box and hitting Enter, your query ends up posted publicly for everyone to see. April 28 in the UK celebrates and commemorates this mistake, with annual Ed Balls Day festivities. #edballsday

- **Sharing your location**. Most social media platforms have a location-based feature which allows you to tag yourself in a certain geographic location. Many also automatically share this location (unless disabled). Generally, it's a rather benign and slightly interesting feature, but there are times when a person's location can give away a great deal of information. In the same way the Twitter CFO's accidental tweet gave away information about a potential acquisition, a person's location could hint at similar information.

In Chapter 18 we'll also discuss some of the risks of getting a bit too merry at the company drinks do and jumping on social media to share your views with the world. Remember that being intoxicated impairs judgement, and often leads people to say things they would not say otherwise. If you're not in a mental state to safely operate a vehicle, think twice about whether you should be operating a social media account.

Oversharing is not always about deliberately sharing too much. However social media companies are set up to collect and share a great deal of data – and that data can sometimes reveal information that a company or their social media manager may not wish to make publicly known.

Conclusion

Social media is a great place to get the message out about your business. There are countless opportunities and methods for sharing content, information and talking with interested people about your products and services. It may be tempting to overindulge and share too much, too often.

Just because you can put anything out into cyberspace does not always mean that it is wise to do so. It's very important that when businesses are putting out its messaging on social media that all related content is clear and cohesive.

Notes

1 Can your social media profile kill your job prospects? www.bbc.co.uk/news/business-42621920 (archived at https://perma.cc/HSV3-DBWN)
2 Facebook snooping on candidates? GDPR could put a stop to that: www.personneltoday.com/hr/facebook-snooping-candidates-gdpr-put-stop/ (archived at https://perma.cc/J7BC-DU7D)
3 Number of employers using social media to screen candidates at all-time high, finds latest CareerBuilder study: http://press.careerbuilder.com/2017-06-15-Number-of-Employers-Using-Social-Media-to-Screen-Candidates-at-All-Time-High-Finds-Latest-CareerBuilder-Study (archived at https://perma.cc/R7V8-3V2S)

4   HMV employees go on Twitter rampage while being fired: http://nymag.com/
    intelligencer/2013/01/hmv-twitter-fired-social-media.html (archived at
    https://perma.cc/82QX-Q9Q7)

5   Twitter executive mistakenly tweets about M&A plans: www.telegraph.co.uk/
    finance/newsbysector/mediatechnologyandtelecoms/11252260/Twitter-
    executive-mistakenly-tweets-about-MandA-plans.html (archived at
    https://perma.cc/Z6U7-PF3Q)

6   Google hit with £44m GDPR fine over ads: www.bbc.co.uk/news/
    technology-46944696 (archived at https://perma.cc/2HYG-7UQ3)

SOCIAL MEDIA CANNOT BE DONE WELL IN-HOUSE

*Working collaboratively with experts to co-create
as and when required is how futurists and thought leaders
describe the 'future of work'.*

Introduction

As social media has become mainstream, organizations have invested not only in setting up accounts and profiles, but also in the human capital necessary to manage social media activities such as content and creative campaign development, social listening, social data analytics and insight and day-to-day community management.

Depending on the shape and structure of the organization, social media activity may fall within the remit of a dedicated social media team or under a broader business unit, such as marketing.

As activity on social channels has become increasingly important for businesses – supporting insights, customer service, brand reputation, brand awareness and consumer purchasing behaviour – so, too, has expertise in how to use the channels effectively become more sought after. It's unlikely that brands that once upon a time would have passed their social media accounts to a willing intern would do so now.

In a relatively short period of time, social media management has become a niche area of expertise. Business schools and marketing institutes now offer specific qualifications just in social media, and just a few years ago mainstream job titles such as 'social media strategist' and 'social media manager' didn't exist.

This leaves many organizations, Chief Marketing Officers and heads of departments wondering whether social media is best managed in-house or outsourced to an external specialist agency.

In this chapter, we'll explore the strengths and weaknesses of both options, and pose some questions for you to consider with the aim of helping you to gain clarity on this quandary.

In-house team or outsourced solution?

Social media activity isn't purely about scheduling posts and simply 'filling the feeds'. There's a whole of lot of strategic thinking, brand messaging and creative campaign alignment required. If you think about it, every interaction, every tweet, response, image, video or advertisement on social media is a brand touchpoint, and due to the nature of the channels, these can be:

- sharing brand messaging
- promoting products or services
- responding to customer queries, viewpoints or engagement on your posts
- tracking conversations, brand mentions, reputation and sentiment
- watching what others in your arena are doing – key partners, competitors, customers and influencers
- managing targeting social advertising campaigns, engagement and conversation
- social selling, using the channels for business development and networking
- recruitment and employer brand messaging

As you can see from this list (which is by no means exhaustive), when thinking how to best manage your social media presence, there will be different projects, some of which will can be managed in-house and some outsourced. It may be that while day-to-day brand promotion and community management is managed internally, paid social advertising campaigns may be sent out of house to an agency.

It helps to be clear on what you want to achieve and, importantly, whether the activity you're looking to embark upon is long-term or short-term. To help determine whether and what to outsource, think about the following:

- How much time do you/your team have to devote to managing social media?
- Do you have the required level of expertise in-house?
- What is it that you are specifically looking for an external agency to achieve (content strategy, creative and development; social media strategy and planning; data, reporting or analytics)? Do you have clarity on the brief?
- Is what you're looking for generalist or specialist? For example: paid advertising on social media or data insights and social media reputation analysis.
- What is the size of your budget? Do you have the scope to increase your headcount or invest in training your current team?
- Is there appetite for the necessary skill development within the team?
- How quickly are you needing to get things started? What's going to fit best with timescales?
- Have you weighed up the pros and cons associated with managing social media activity in-house vs outsourcing it?

Time is one of the biggest reasons businesses look to outsource their social media. Being a socially connected business is a 24/7 effort. Keeping your brand in front of customers means consistently dripping content and messages and being responsive. Customers choose to engage at a time that suits them and, as we've discussed in earlier chapters, expectations around the speed of response are high.

Your authentic voice

Just as a CEO or leader can't outsource their own voice in order to build trust (see Chapter 12), authenticity of voice needs to be considered at the brand and organizational level too.

Whether you are training a team member to manage social media or outsourcing to an external agency or freelancer, it's critical that a rigorous induction-style process is implemented. In just the same way as if a new team member were being welcomed to the business, your external agency needs to know your brand guidelines, what they can and can't say, the tone of voice you use, and any dos and don'ts. Like any induction process, it takes time and a bit of mentoring to ensure that the necessary learning is embedded.

Once a decision has been made, don't make the mistake of not staying close to what's being said on your social platforms. Learning and trust is something that grows – and blaming your community manager never goes down well.

US fast food chain Wendy's experienced this in 2016, when they posted a picture of Pepe the Frog on their Twitter feed – a meme which had evolved to represent white supremacy. Wendy's often gets their tone of voice just right and is well respected for their witty Twitter engagement, yet there was considerable backlash towards this tweet. Wendy's apologized and deleted the tweet, saying that their community manager was 'unaware of the connotations'.

Sense-checks and approval

The other point the Wendy's example above raises is the necessity of carrying out quick sense-checks before posting, or even implementing a more formal approval and sign off process.

Enterprise social media dashboard tools (as mentioned in Chapter 2) such as Hootsuite, Buffer, Sprout Social or CoSchedule enable agencies or in-house teams to share proposed scheduled messages with an approver, so that they can review, edit or make suggestions around language and brand messaging.

Over time, the intention is that those managing the messaging become familiar with tone of voice and what is and isn't permissible, and it may be that the initial approval process becomes more relaxed, with only periodic sense-checks. This may take the form of the community manager, whether internal or agency-side, sending a quick message on Skype or WhatsApp to check the tone before scheduling. Had this happened at Wendy's, Pepe would have been captured before being released to the world at large.

Of course, if disaster strikes, there's always the 'delete' option – but, again, this requires speedy lines of communication and responsiveness.

Hybrid collaborative solution

It may be that you need to bring in external expertise for specific campaigns – to run an audit of where you are with your current social media activity, to help develop a broader social media strategy or to support those campaigns where you don't have in-house competence, for example.

A hybrid collaborative solution enables you either train up your team to give them the competence or to work in partnership with an agency on a campaign or project for an agreed period of time. This model can also be really useful in imparting knowledge to internal team members.

Pros and cons

Whether hybrid, in-house or outsourced, the route you choose will be fully dependent on the size and structure of your business, budgets and desired outcome. We've highlighted a few pros and cons.

The pros of staying in-house

- employees are already clear on brand message, values and dos and don'ts – they live and breathe the brand every day
- the ability to make changes and respond in real time
- the opportunity for new content development, picking up the latest internal news and developments
- employees know the customer and already understand how to engage with them

The cons of in-house management

- existing staff may not have the time, manpower or expertise
- employees can develop tunnel vision – failing to think outside the box and bring creative angles to activities
- employees may be restricted by internal politics
- you will need to invest in enterprise technologies such as social media management dashboards, analytics or social listening and sentiment analysis tools

The pros of outsourcing

- agencies have a broader view of what works and what doesn't work across different campaigns, accounts and industries
- they have specialist expertise that you can draw upon, and should be up to date with the latest shifts and developments in their industry

- you can buy in the service flexibly, to fit with budgets and campaign requirements

- agencies may come up with more creative, 'out of the box' content ideas

- they will have already invested in the necessary tools and dashboards to facilitate effective management, insight and reporting

The cons of outsourcing

- you will need to induct the external agency or freelancer on your brand messaging, values and dos and don'ts

- effectively, they have to become an extension of your team and so there is an onboarding 'getting to know one another' time period to consider

- there may be some toing and froing between client and agency to make changes and respond in not-so-real time (to eradicate this, processes need to be put in place so that there is opportunity for immediate contact)

- someone within the business will need to be the partner liaison – working with the agency to share latest news stories, content and updates, and generally steer activity

Conclusion

Social media can most certainly be managed well in-house, provided that the organization is structured with a dedicated team and has the necessary resource, expertise and time to commit. If this is the case, then the 'authentic voice' of a business is far better coming directly from within the organization.

In contrast, if the organization isn't equipped to manage social media activity and there isn't the appetite or resource to build an in-house team, then working with an agency in either an outsourced or hybrid capacity offers an effective and often cost-effective solution.

Our view is that the hybrid option offers the most social solution. You can work collaboratively using social technologies to connect, steer and converse and, importantly, keep clear lines of communication open to support speedy responses and ongoing learning.

Working collaboratively with experts to co-create as and when required is how futurists and thought leaders describe the 'future of work'. In *The Future of Work in Technology*, the authors determine that forces of change are affecting three major dimensions of work: the work itself, who does the work, and where work is done.[1]

When we consider the findings in Chapters 6 and 12 around how social media is proving to break down silos within organizations, developing faster and more connected communications, we can also see how these social technologies can be used to break down the outsourced/in-house paradigm by allowing truly social collaboration.

Note

1 The future of work in technology: www2.deloitte.com/content/dam/Deloitte/ec/
   Documents/technology-media-telecommunications/DI_The-future-of-work-in-
   technology%20(1).pdf (archived at https://perma.cc/D78T-S9HW)

MYTH 10

SOCIAL MEDIA IS PURELY FOR BROADCASTING

Social channels provide the opportunity to connect with our audiences and really get to hear the real-world conversations they are having, as they happen – their likes, dislikes, feelings, preferences, gripes, dreams and ideals.

Introduction

When it comes to social media, this myth is still taken literally by far too many people, brands and organizations.

Take a look at random business accounts on Twitter, LinkedIn or Facebook – and you'll often see a stream of promotional, one-way broadcast posts. Consistent, yes! Yet often with zero or very low engagement.

Far from being socially engaged with audiences, it's very clear that the whole purpose of many accounts is purely to broadcast. In fact, the focus on broadcasting overrides any opportunity for genuine engagement – so much so that comments, shares, retweets or other signals of engagement are often totally ignored. Clearly, no one is tasked with monitoring and primed to respond. The two-way conversational aspect of 'being social' just isn't part of the remit.

We refer to this myopic practice as 'broadcasting blindness'. The focus is purely one-way. A series of push communications, machine-gun marketing style; putting the blinkers on and throwing spaghetti at the wall hoping it will stick, albeit consistently, regardless of engagement.

The 80/20 ratio

We like the analogy: two eyes, two ears, and just the one mouth. This approach to broadcasting equates to a ratio of approximately 80 per cent listening and 20 per cent broadcasting. 80 per cent of the time you should be tuned in, responding, elaborating, extending, educating and entertaining, and 20 per cent of the time you are directly promoting.

Yet theory clearly doesn't drive real-world action. A 2016 study by Sprout Social found that brands share 23 promotional messages for every message they respond to.[1] If we extrapolate that to total social media activity, the balance ratio actually equates to 4 per cent of activity focused on responding, and 96 per cent on promotion. A far cry indeed from the theoretical 80/20 balance.

It's clear to see where this myopia emerges from: one-way broadcasting has been used since advertising took off in the 1930s. Promotional methods such as TV advertising, press advertising, trade-press advertorials, magazine editorials, billboard advertising, direct mail and even radio all focus on pushing messages, regardless of whether there's desire from the audience to consume.

When they first came on the scene, social channels were initially simply seen as new channels to market. They were largely adopted by marketing departments and managed as part of the marketing channel mix, being used to extend the broadcast messaging range of campaigns. For some organizations, this marketing-centric focus is still very much the case.

While traditional promotional broadcasting historically focused on linear communications, social media enables networked conversations. A broad range of one-to-one, one-to-many and many-to-many conversations are facilitated, with peers, colleagues, friends, strangers, influencers, brands, organizations, leaders, thought leaders, authors, product developers and even world leaders – a hive of connected conversations.

Beyond broadcasting

Using channels purely to push promotional messages is short-sighted – and ignores the numerous advantages that social media provides. Over the past decade, it's become apparent that social media channels offer organizations and brands a huge focus group to tap into. In 2013, Crimson Hexagon's survey of digital marketing professionals revealed that nearly three-quarters (72 per cent) believed monitoring public sentiment via social media is just as good, if not better, than using traditional focus groups.[2] Meltwater's 2017 article agrees: 'When you've got two billion active Facebook users a month ready and waiting to give you their opinion, the focus group doesn't stand a chance.'[3]

Social networks provide the scope for customer insight that if seen 15–20 years would have been met with jaw-dropping awe. Tuning in and listening via social media presents significant opportunity for organizations. However, when there's too much emphasis on pushing out promotional messages, these chances to engage with customers are lost.

Listening to customers and developing two-way conversations will allow any organization to develop their operations in the following areas.

Customer service

It's commonplace for brands and organizations to manage customer queries and complaints via social media channels. This ranges from supermarkets to public transport services, police services, hospital services, doctors and schools, and large corporations through to microbusinesses. Many often have dedicated accounts, sitting separately to their core brand accounts. The remit is solely to serve the customer service purpose.

The Sprout Social report mentioned identifies that when it comes to customer service, around a third of people prefer to reach out to organizations via social media rather than call them, visit their website or use live chat. That same report also highlights the somewhat disturbing findings that 89 per cent of such messages to organizations are totally ignored!

Companies have to put these social media channels in place to serve their audiences – but the reality is that far too many are actually failing to truly tune in, listen and respond. As Scott Stratten and Alison Kramer succinctly put it in their book *UnMarketing*: 'It's like turning up to a networking event wearing earplugs.'[4]

Brand and relationship building

Failure to respond to customer queries doesn't just ignore the need to serve the customer and develop positive brand value – it also misses the opportunity to build and strengthen relationships with customers. This is a fundamental requirement for business success. How impressed would you be by a brand or organization if you shared your opinion with them or asked them a question, and received zero response?

What better way is there of engaging with people than by letting them know you are listening and that their views, issues, gripes and insights matter? We all want, and increasingly expect, to be heard. It's not just about mutual respect, however; it's also good for business.

Customer service statistics gathered by Helpscout bring to light the impact of positive and negative brand experiences.[5] On the negative side:

- 88 per cent of consumers aren't as likely to buy from companies who don't answer their complaints.

- It takes 12 good experiences to make up for one bad experience.

- Unhappy customers will tell between 9 and 15 people about a bad experience.

- 30 per cent of customers who are shunned by brands on social media are more likely to switch to a competitor.

On the positive side:

- Customers who feel engaged by companies on social medial will spend up to 40 per cent more with them than other customers.

- 81 per cent are more likely to buy from a business again after a good service experience.

You'd think these statistics alone (and there are many others) would ensure social monitoring and tuning into audiences was considered a priority for businesses.

Listening is gold

There are billions of messages shared on social platforms each day:[6,7]

- 4.2 billion likes on Instagram posts
- 500 million tweets

- 60 billion messages across Facebook and WhatsApp
- 30,000 long-form posts on LinkedIn

The data is beyond big and the volume of real-time conversation is staggering, providing a significant amounts of insight and sentiment for research teams, agencies and organizations to analyse and draw valuable business intelligence from.

The opportunity for listening, whether at a sophisticated or basic level, is readily available. As discussed in Chapter 2, sophisticated enterprise solutions are available to help organizations uncover sentiment and carry out competitor analysis, such as Brandwatch, Meltwater and Hootsuite, as well as basic keyword tracking tools such as Google Alerts and directly using advanced search functions on the native social media platforms.

Listening can assist with a number of highly practical insights:

- **Customer sentiment** – how your customers are feeling, what they're talking about, where and when they participate.
- **Corporate messaging** – the ability to listen and respond to sentiment appropriately, whether that's defending your brand's position, educating your audiences from a thought leadership perspective, mitigating potential brand damage or engaging audiences on a topic that's close to their hearts.
- **Competitor sentiment** – watching what your competitors are saying, and the response sentiment of their audiences (useful for opportunity spotting), as well as measuring your share of voice against your competitors. In an interview one of the authors conducted with John Legere, CEO of TMobile US, he described how tuning into competitors and the conversations audiences are having with them helps him to drive innovation around new product development.[8]
- **Brand awareness and share of voice** – gaining a general understanding of your positioning in the marketplace.
- **Brand sentiment** – finding out how people feel about your brand.
- **Product development** – people may be having conversations about how your product or service performs. Innovation and development ideas can be gleaned directly from those actively using the product. Use your customers to learn how you can improve the user experience – who better to give you insights than those already using and talking about your products?

- **Influencer relationship development** – when you are listening, you can find out who the influential people are in your networks; the ones consistently sharing and advocating your products into their networks, helping to amplify your brand and awareness generally. Identifying such influencers, thanking them, and potentially developing relationships with them can provide a smart way to continuously optimize reach and influence in an authentic way.

While most listening on social media focuses on brand mentions – those instances where users have tagged a brand or an organization – it's also worth tracking misspelled or generic (untagged) mentions of your brand or organization name.

Social listening within the organization

Whether adopting enterprise social networking systems or creating their own proprietary social networks, more and more organizations are using social technologies as internal communication platforms (which we'll explore more closely in Chapter 13). Here, the same listening principles apply.

As with consumers, if an organization simply considers social networking as a platform for corporate communications, broadcasting and pushing out promotional messages in a linear way to internal audiences, then this misses the point of connected, social, networked conversations. Failures may include not optimizing collaboration between employees across departments, or not hearing from team members that may not ordinarily feel comfortable raising their hand or sharing ideas in an open forum.

Companies should ensure that there are processes and systems in place to listen to employees and sentiment. And it's equally important to respond in a timely and productive way to encourage continuous authentic engagement, relationship development and overall success. 2018 findings from Novartis suggest a 12 per cent increase in employee satisfaction after implementing social media to engage and connect with staff.[9]

Another study highlights findings from Starbucks and L'Oréal.[10] Starbucks is named as one of the most engaged brands, citing an increase in share price due to increased level of employee engagement, and L'Oréal report an overwhelming amount of employee engagement and goodwill generated by getting their teams involved with an internal campaign.

Conclusion

Social channels are highly practical for reaching new audiences, brand building and sharing messages – but let's not forget that they are networks. They are not one-way broadcast channels; they facilitate connected conversations.

The importance of listening shouldn't be underestimated. Listening is a basic human function, a key sense that aids survival. It's equally relevant for business survival. Focused listening helps inform what you broadcast, so that your communications and content are more useful and purposeful and your audiences are compelled to engage.

Listening, hearing, and, importantly, acknowledging and responding shows your audiences, whether internal or external, that you care enough to respond. Such acknowledgment is profoundly impactful. Conversely, if someone is talking to you and you ignore them, they will eventually give up and find another organization who is interested in what they have to say.

Social media technologies give you the opportunity to tune into your customers, to broaden your audience and reach those you may not ordinarily have the chance to connect with; to build and strengthen relationships and harness knowledge and insights.

The myth that social media is purely for broadcasting your organization's messages is not true. The bulk of activity should ideally focus where the gold lies – and that's in the listening. Social channels provide the opportunity to connect with our audiences and really get to hear the real-world conversations they are having, as they happen – their likes, dislikes, feelings, preferences, gripes, dreams and ideals.

And of course, social media activity isn't the same across the board (another myth we busted in Chapter 3). People use the array of social channels for different reasons. Understanding the how, when and what of social network usage also helps you to understand where and what to listen for.

Knowing how to get people's attention, grow your audience, entertain and sell products and services can all be informed by listening. It's better to respond with a meaningful answer than to push out hyperbole that no one engages with.

Very simply, don't make social media all about you – but, instead, all about them.

Notes

1 The Sprout Social Index, Edition VI: Shunning your customers on social? https://sproutsocial.com/insights/data/q2-2016/ (archived at https://perma.cc/7WMA-Z52N)

2 72% of professionals see social media as a more reliable source of public sentiment than traditional focus groups: www.thedrum.com/news/2013/10/15/72-professionals-see-social-media-more-reliable-source-public-sentiment-traditional (archived at https://perma.cc/J9KY-74ZQ)

3 Focus groups are dead, thanks to social media: https://mumbrella.com.au/social-media-was-the-final-nail-in-the-focus-groups-coffin-462210 (archived at https://perma.cc/5AZY-78CN)

4 Stratten, S and Kramer, A (2012) *UnMarketing: Stop marketing. Start engaging*, Wiley, Chichester

5 75 customer service facts quotes and statistics: www.helpscout.com/75-customer-service-facts-quotes-statistics/ (archived at https://perma.cc/GKD8-YLJP)

6 22+ Instagram stats that marketers can't ignore this year: https://blog.hootsuite.com/instagram-statistics/ (archived at https://perma.cc/CJA9-WZJR)

7 126 amazing social media statistics and facts: www.brandwatch.com/blog/amazing-social-media-statistics-and-facts/ (archived at https://perma.cc/6KEH-ZD76)

8 Carvill, M (2018) *Get Social – Social media strategy and tactics for leaders*, Kogan Page, London

9 Social media proves to boost employee engagement: www.forbes.com/sites/forbesagencycouncil/2018/02/13/social-media-proves-to-boost-employee-engagement/ (archived at https://perma.cc/J9Z4-76BJ)

10 Embracing social media as a means to achieve employee engagement: www.hrexchangenetwork.com/employee-engagement/articles/embracing-social-media-as-a-means-to-achieve (archived at https://perma.cc/Z46V-EFCY)

SOCIAL MEDIA REPLACES REAL-LIFE NETWORKING

Social networking certainly doesn't replace face-to-face networking, but rather plays both a lead role and a supportive role – helping you to start and deepen relationships.

Introduction

When evaluating this myth, it's worth us revisiting the very beginning of social media.

Step back just shy of two decades to when they first began: LinkedIn in 2002, Facebook 2004 and Twitter 2006. At this time, each platform was regularly referred to as a 'social networking' platform. In fact, in their own biographies they still are.

The focus at the outset was mainly about connecting with friends, family and social networking – making new connections, digitally. Effectively, it was old-school networking revisited online.

Over time, the term 'social media' has become synonymous with all that we do on these pioneering platforms and the other social networks that joined them, such as Instagram and Snapchat (2010 and 2011 respectively).

The evolution of the social media platforms since their networking foundations includes the development of sophisticated advertising methodologies – the ability to supply timely content and advertisements straight into the palms of highly targeted audiences. Paid social media has become a central part of social media activity, not only aligned with ecommerce potential, but also to help brands and organizations optimize their reach. Brands and organizations are no longer wholly reliant on organic networked conversations, referrals and sharing amongst their followers to amplify their messages, as they can now take advantage of a range of advertising options to target audiences directly.

In this chapter, we'll consider the values of traditional networking and consider the ongoing debate around whether social networking replaces traditional networking – or whether they're the perfect complementary partners.

Both sides of the argument

There's an ongoing debate around whether social networking websites replace face-to-face interaction. Interestingly, this is taking place entirely online – you can visit the debate at Debate.org.[1] At the time of writing you'll find the results sitting at 55 per cent No (the platforms aren't replacing face-to-face interaction), and 45 per cent Yes (they are). And while it's currently pretty close, there's also plenty of commentary around the pros and cons from both sides of the argument.

To summarize a few comments from the Yes voters, social media:

- enables those that wouldn't ordinarily speak up in a room due to shyness to air their views
- enables connection with a wider community that people wouldn't ordinarily have access to
- enables people to access and explore wider viewpoints without the constraint of geography
- gives access to more opinion and expertise, help and advice
- enables people to use their time more effectively and stay in tune with people they don't ordinarily have time to

If you visit the debate, you'll notice that there's consensus even amongst the Yes voters that meeting face to face is generally better. There is also general agreement that face-to-face meetings aren't always possible, and that social networks can help fill that void and enable connectivity and collaboration, albeit remotely, where otherwise there may have been a total loss of communication.

Among the No voters, the view is largely that social networks can't replace physical networks. Yet there's still a consistent level of positivity around the role of social media. Social networks are deemed to be really useful for keeping in touch with friends and family and staying up to date. However, the view is that social media doesn't, and shouldn't, totally replace physical interaction with fellow humans.

To summarize a few comments from the No side:

- People aren't really themselves on social media – they're not talking about real problems, but rather just showing all the good stuff. It's not a true representation.

- It's easy for things to be taken out of context – because there's not the physical connection of a smile, or the opportunity to hear the tone of voice.

- People can become so addicted to virtual life that they forget real life.

- People are more invested in the meeting when that meeting takes place face to face.

All these arguments are valid, with even the No campaign speaking favourably about the role of social networks in supporting relationships. This led us to explore the strength of online relationships, and whether a relationship that starts online is weaker than one that starts face to face.

Online and offline relationships

A 2017 MIT Technology Review study found that when personal relationships start online, they may have an advantage over relationships that start in real life.[2] The report focused on a body of research which has been studying the concept of social networks for 50 years. It shows that real social networks are those where people are strongly connected to a relatively small group of neighbours and only loosely connect to more distant people. (We liken this to friends and family and acquaintances.)

In the study, the 'loose connections' turn out to be extremely important, serving as a bridge between our close friends and other groups, enabling us to connect with a wider community.

From the personal relationship perspective, it's the loose connections that have traditionally played a key role in meeting our partners. While most people were unlikely to date one of their best friends, they were highly likely to date people who they met though a friend of a friend. In the language of network theory, dating partners were embedded in one another's networks.

Turning to the online networks, then, the report explores how online dating has changed that language of network theory – for the better. People that meet online tend to be complete strangers – and when people meet in this way, it sets up social links that were previously non-existent. There are many benefits being reaped due to the introduction of these new social links – one being that it offers a broader opportunity to break away from the potential confines of our own local networks.

Another interesting finding from the research is that married couples who meet online have lower rates of marital break-up than those who meet through more traditional avenues. This is likely due to the fact that selection criteria within social networks are quite targeted, so those meeting tend to share more of the same values.

Parallels with business networking

While we couldn't find any similar studies that have been formally carried out in the business arena, given that we're all human beings, from a relationship development perspective, we can use this lens to look at the development of business relationships. In just the same way that social networks are facilitating new social links that wouldn't ordinarily happen in the dating world, so too are they facilitating new links in the business world. For example, platforms such as CoFounders Lab help those seeking business partners to access over 400,000 potential matches.[3]

David Mata, cofounder of Blockbits Capital, met his business partner via Facebook according to a 2018 Fundera article.[4] It includes a quote from David expressing how similar the two were in personality, thinking, values and focus – similar aspects to those outlined in the online dating study. The online pairing creating a successful business partnership, reporting a market value of £29.5 million.

Networking has always played a significant role in business development. LinkedIn, probably the social network most synonymous with online business networking, focuses its entire platform on helping business people to connect, expand and strengthen their professional networks.

It operates a tiered level of connection – primary connections, secondary connections and third-tier connections. Primary connections are those in your immediate network – these may be your peers, people you regularly do business with, or people you've met and have decided to connect with for ongoing conversation and future opportunity. The secondary network are those that your primary network are connected to, and the third tier are those that are yet to be reached through your network.

LinkedIn provides clear visibility of where people sit in your network. For example, let's say, you're at a business event and you meet someone. You decide to connect with them on LinkedIn, search for them on the platform, and see that they are a secondary connection, already connected to your sales director. Immediately, this gives you the opportunity to open a conversation about the strength and context of that relationship.

This feature can also be useful for making network connections more indirectly. Using the same example, let's say you're at that business event, and you see someone speaking on stage. You decide they would be a great connection for business development. You don't know them, you haven't spoken to them, yet when you search for them on the platform, you notice that your sales director is already connected to them. You could then ask your sales director to introduce the two of you – in just the same way they may make an introduction offline.

Social selling

It's easy to see how the visibility of connections online can expand opportunity for building new links via social networks for business. This is commonly referred to as 'social selling', the act of leveraging your social network connections to find the right prospects, build trusted relationships and to ultimately leverage those relationships to achieve business objectives and sales targets.

Effectively, it's simply good old-fashioned business networking and building trust – but doing so purely online. The social networks enable businesses to keep in touch with clients, partners and potential clients regularly, eradicating the awkward cold call – and, again, without the challenge of location.

LinkedIn's 2018 State of Sales report claims that 90 per cent of top performing sales-people now use social media as part of their sales strategy.[5] And for sales representatives that do invest in social media, 64 per cent of them hit their team quota – compared to only 49 per cent that don't use social media.

While new social links can start out loosely over weeks, months and sometimes years of networking, collaborating, sharing and conversing online, those loose links strengthen and build to become stronger, more meaningful networks which are often clustered around the founding topic or interest.

As authors, we've been conversing on the topic of social media on Twitter using the hashtag #socialceo, which has resulted in moving relationships from online to offline interviews, meetings and collaboration. This is a simple example of loose connections talking about the same topic coming together to strengthen connections into something far more significant than a collection of tweets.

In just the same way as those romantic partners that meet online are proving to have stronger foundations and longer marriages, so too can coming together with likeminded individuals online serve towards a more successful, purposeful business network.

In 2018 the Internet Society shared their '25 under 25' awardees– 25 online community networks started by people under the age of 25, which are making a difference around the world bringing like-minded communities together.[6] It's an inspiring list of networks, covering health education, cyber-bullying, digital activism, crowdsourcing, teaching IT skills and matching farmers with vendors.

Moving from online to offline (without the awkwardness)

Some people love face-to-face networking. They happily attend events with the objective of making as many connections as possible. For others, break times at events with facilitated 'space to network' can be an excruciatingly awkward affair causing people to bury their heads in their phones or spend a little longer than necessary in the bathroom.

When it comes to moving from online to offline networking, it's always a little less socially awkward to meet with someone you've been talking to online. There's already a shared sense of 'knowing them' – the icebreakers have happened, and you're often into a different level of conversation.

Research in Science Daily supports this notion, showing that the online world is now increasingly facilitating new relationships in the offline world.[7]

It's useful at this point to address your own use of online and offline networking – and reflect on the realities. While you may have hundreds or perhaps thousands of connections online, it's highly likely that you're in regular contact with only a few people at any one time.

Those conversations and connections are generally clustered around a shared interest or topic. And if you join in a conversation around a shared interest or topic, it may be that you find yourself interacting with a new 'social link' – who just so happens to be on the same wavelength or has a slightly different view which you find interesting – and so you connect. What starts online may even evolve into a long-standing, relevant and strong relationship, or, as in the case of BlockBits Capital and many others, a new business venture.

Conclusion

Social networking certainly doesn't replace face-to-face networking, but rather plays both a lead role and a supportive role – helping you to start and deepen relationships, either via continuous conversations, shared initiatives (either online or offline) or a move towards face-to-face meetings or even a collaborative project.

In the same way that dating agencies 'match' values and personality to check if the chemistry works, there's no denying that the online social networks enable you to 'match' values, ideas and opportunities. From a business perspective, these networks enable you to stay connected and aligned with clients, partners and prospective clients – complementing your face-to-face networking activity, deepening and strengthening those all-important relationships.

Notes

1 Can social networks replace face-to-face interaction? www.debate.org/opinions/can-social-networking-websites-replace-face-to-face-interaction (archived at https://perma.cc/KCX6-NTXZ)

2 First evidence that online dating is changing the nature of society: www.technologyreview.com/s/609091/first-evidence-that-online-dating-is-changing-the-nature-of-society/ (archived at https://perma.cc/598H-XDQS)

3 CoFounders Lab: www.cofounderslab.com (archived at https://perma.cc/9Z53-49SX)

4 Should you start a business with someone you met online? www.fundera.com/blog/start-a-business-with-someone-you-met-online (archived at https://perma.cc/FG4R-MY6V)

5 The State of Sales 2018: https://business.linkedin.com/sales-solutions/b2b-sales-strategy-guides/the-state-of-sales-2018 (archived at https://perma.cc/H7DV-7YHD)

6 25 under 25 awardees: www.internetsociety.org/25th/25-under-25/awardees (archived at https://perma.cc/3J9E-G889)

7 Online and offline: The changing face of meetings: www.sciencedaily.com/releases/2015/03/150309082814.htm (archived at https://perma.cc/HHY2-NL5G)

SOCIAL MEDIA MEANS MY BUSINESS HAS TO BE AVAILABLE 24/7

*In order to manage brand reputation, build relationships with
your customers and grow the bottom line through customer
service, being responsive and conscious of the time
it takes to respond is key.*

Introduction

When it comes to understanding how available your business needs to be on social media, a few factors come into play:

- Which social media channels do you need to be active on? This comes down to understanding where your audiences or customers are, and analysing their chosen tools of communication.

- Understanding how those channels are used by your audiences, the time they spend on the channels, and typical activity.

- A fundamental understanding of why you want to have a presence on the channels. This is probably the most important thing to consider.

The answer to why you want to have a social media presence should be more than simply: 'because everyone else has'. And yes, while it's difficult to find organizations these days that don't have some form of social presence, the decision to participate, and how, should be aligned with the strategic direction of your business and effectively resourced.

Remember, no one is forcing your business to be on social media; it's a case of figuring out what works for your business and is necessary for its continued success. And if your customers and key audiences are using these channels day-to-day as a preferred method of communication, then why wouldn't you want to engage them? Particularly when you consider some of the positive aspects of doing so.

In this chapter, we'll explore how people are using social media channels, changing customer expectation levels and the opportunity for setting clear expectations for your audiences. We'll also share insights about the evolving automation technologies, tools and resources that can help you to manage the practicalities of being readily available to your audiences, helping you to consider your position on being always-on, 24/7.

How your audience uses social media

As we've highlighted throughout this book, social media is inseparable from our everyday lives. We discussed access statistics and typical usage in Chapter 2 – but to reiterate, 3.196 billion people are actively using social media networks on a day-to-day basis. The latest statistics from Ofcom, the UK's regulatory media body, show that people's online time is growing by around 7 per cent annually.[1] The average UK adult spent 3 hours 15 minutes per day online in 2018 – a rise of 11 minutes since 2017. This translates to 1,192 hours over the year; the equivalent of around 50 days on the internet.

Globally, it's reported that the average social media user spends 2 hours and 16 minutes each day on social platforms, up one minute from 2018.[2] This equates to approximately one third of total internet time, and one seventh of our waking lives.

Time spent on social media varies considerably for different cultures. For example, internet users in Japan spend an average of 36 minutes on social media each day, whereas, at the other extreme, Filipinos average four hours and twelve minutes.

While some specific channels will dominate in different countries, it's likely that the places where all your customers participate, at least some of the time, will include Facebook, Facebook Messenger, YouTube, WhatsApp, Instagram, Twitter, Snapchat and LinkedIn.

As to time spent on each channel, a 2019 report from TechJury[3] identifies the following average usage analysis, based on what people did in 2018:

- Facebook – 58 minutes a day (on the mobile Facebook app)
- YouTube – one hour a day (on a mobile device)
- Facebook Messenger – 9.36 minutes per day
- WhatsApp – 28.4 minutes a day
- Instagram – 5 minutes a day
- Twitter – 2.7 minutes a day
- Linkedin – 17 minutes per month[4]
- Snapchat – 34.5 minutes a day[5]

These statistics give you an indication of average usage, but to get an accurate understanding of your own audience, we recommend you undertake your own analysis. We found there to be a huge number of differing research findings in this area – which are influenced by a range of variables. For example, we know that younger demographics use social media platforms for longer periods of time than older ones.

Various technologies can help you learn more about your audiences, their sentiments and platform preferences. Analytical tools such as BuzzRadar, Brandwatch, Meltwater and others offer sophisticated deeper insight. You can also explore the basic analytics provided by each of the native social platforms. For example, Facebook's Insights tool can be extremely informative, and LinkedIn can also provide audience insights, particularly if you have the respective tracking pixels embedded in your website.

What customers want

Let's now look at what customers expect when a business positions itself as being accessible via social media.

Social platforms have been inextricably linked with customer service and support since their inception, and while these platforms have evolved considerably since those beginnings, customer service is still a significant part of social media engagement for organizations. In fact, many organizations have consciously manoeuvred their first line of customer service response to be delivered via Facebook and Twitter. This is discussed in more detail in Chapter 6.

Let's consider a brand or organization that would ordinarily expect high levels of customer service interaction for complaints, such as wireless carrier solution TMobile. Their social platforms show that they make use of both Facebook via a Facebook Messenger chatbot service, and Twitter, with a dedicated @TMobileHelp account to connect and communicate directly with customers.

It's unusual now to find any organization with a customer-facing component that isn't taking advantage of these channels. Supermarkets, transport providers, retail brands, public services, governments, products, service solutions – even if the available social platforms aren't positioned as dedicated support services, empowered customers will instinctively use the channels to raise queries.

A 2018 *Harvard Business Review* article highlights the bottom-line impact of customer responsiveness via social media.[6] Using data from Twitter, the research team set out to test the hypothesis that those customers who have a positive interaction via social media will reward that brand with greater loyalty or will pay a premium price for the product or service.

The research experiment ran across two service industries where there was scope for a significant number of interactions: airlines and wireless carriers. They took a sample of over 400,000 customer service-related tweets comprising complaints, questions and comments and monitored progress. Six months after the customers had tweeted the various companies, they were invited to take a brief survey.

The outcomes of the research showed that:

- customers who had interacted with a brand's customer service representative on Twitter were significantly more likely to spend extra with the brand or choose the brand more often
- customers who received any kind of response were willing to pay more
- net promoter scores were improved

What is interesting to note was the reaction to receiving any kind of response. This indicates that even a response that wasn't resolving the issue, but simply acknowledging it, was still likely to improve the brand relationship.

Response time is also key

The *Harvard Business Review* study also measured response time. This is an important metric. It found that good service happens fast – and when responses were received within five minutes or less, the customer was willing to pay more.

When it comes to expectation around response times, five minutes may seem unrealistic. However, it depends on the level of response given; remember that any response is better than no response. In the first instance, an automated acknowledgment or question could be offered.

It's reported that 67 per cent of consumers have engaged with a brand via social media for customer service needs – and yet, while we're using social media as a key customer support communication channel, our customer service expectations don't appear to be being met.[7] Further, HubSpot reports that 80 per cent of customers expect brands to respond to their social media posts within 24 hours, with 50 per cent of customers claiming that they would cease doing business with a company that failed to respond to their negative social media post.[8]

For any organization, it's worth responding – not only to turn around that negative situation as quickly as possible and retain that customer, but also to avoid others being influenced by such posts. According to the HubSpot piece, 62 per cent of customers say they are influenced by negative social media comments about a brand, to the extent that they would cease doing business with them, even if they personally didn't have a negative experience.

Enter artificial intelligence

While response times required may need to be quicker than those typically delivered via traditional routes, there's also the volume of potential interactions to consider. Increasingly, artificial intelligence chatbots are being used to engage, filter and create more efficiencies to improve customer service enquiries, far more quickly than could be managed by human customer service agents.

A great example is Facebook's Messenger Chatbot, a friendly and accessible automated messaging software that converses with customers, which can be programmed to understand questions, provide answers and execute tasks such as loading a web page, routing to join a call or sharing a file to download. As well as speedily responding to customers, this automation of information gathering and management of menial tasks frees up time for customer service agents to focus on more involved enquiries.

Another great solution is Cora, the Royal Bank of Scotland's intelligent chatbot.[9] Cora has been programmed to manage over 200 customer intentions and has more than a thousand responses. It's estimated that Cora answers 5,000 questions a day and understands when 'she' needs to pass the customer across to a human agent – who by then has a documented understanding of the conversation, so they're able to assist more speedily.

Setting clear expectations

Of course, while there's an assumption that just by having a presence on social media means that you are accessible 24/7, brands and organizations can still manage customer expectation by providing clarity as to when platforms are staffed. For example, the Marks and Spencer Twitter account, @ marksandspencer, states very clearly in the header of their bio, the hours that their social media accounts are available:

> 'Welcome to the official M&S Twitter page. Follow us here for news on our
> newest food, latest fashion and home inspiration. We're here daily, 8am-10pm.'

Such clarity at least gives the customer the understanding that if they send a message at 11 am at night, it's unlikely anyone will respond until the morning.

Conclusion

While the myth of needing to be available 24/7 isn't totally busted, the reality is that while there is an always-on mentality, and social media channels are accessed by billions of people for a growing number of hours per day, your business has full permission to be accessible and engaged in a way that fits with your operating processes.

However, when you are on social channels, in order to manage brand reputation, build relationships with your customers and grow the bottom line through customer service, being responsive and conscious of the time it takes to respond is key.

We've identified that some organizations, where it fits with brand and audience, are using social media channels for 24/7 front-line customer service – for example, American Airlines. The official Twitter for the world's largest airline states: 'We're here 24/7 for #AATeam kudos or travel concerns. For a formal response, visit ...'

For others, they've made it very clear when they are and are not available. We've also discussed some of the automated tools that enable you to manage engagement beyond the restraints of physical headcount or out of hours. The reality is that customer service management via social media channels is a significant component of how you serve your customers – and with the right intention, clarity of expectation and intelligent resources, you can manage your social media presence, in a way that fits with your operations, on your terms.

Notes

1 People's online experiences revealed: www.ofcom.org.uk/about-ofcom/latest/media/media-releases/2019/peoples-online-experiences-revealed (archived at https://perma.cc/U44J-226P)

2 Digital in 2019: https://wearesocial.com/global-digital-report-2019 (archived at https://perma.cc/92PZ-N493)

3 How long do people spend on social media? https://techjury.net/blog/time-spent-on-social-media/ (archived at https://perma.cc/38M4-DGYX)

4 46 eye-opening LinkedIn statistics for 2019: https://99firms.com/blog/linkedin-statistics/#gref (archived at https://perma.cc/9ZSX-7WWU)

5 38 interesting and fascinating Snapchat statistics: www.brandwatch.com/blog/snapchat-statistics/ (archived at https://perma.cc/KDP3-7YYA)

6 How customer service can turn angry customers into loyal ones: https://hbr.org/2018/01/how-customer-service-can-turn-angry-customers-into-loyal-ones (archived at https://perma.cc/ADN8-2U5E)

7 6 key elements of using social media for customer service: https://freshsparks.com/using-social-media-for-customer-service (archived at https://perma.cc/9TCB-HUP6)

8 What are your customers' expectations for social media response time? https://blog.hubspot.com/service/social-media-response-time (archived at https://perma.cc/L3Z8-2BVX)

9 Raising Cora: www.ibm.com/industries/banking-financial-markets/front-office/chatbots-banking (archived at https://perma.cc/KMZ5-LSDA)

MYTH 13

SOCIAL MEDIA IS NO USE FOR INTERNAL COMMUNICATIONS

While social networks were originally developed to enable people to connect and broadcast externally, the benefits have been appropriated to help organizations with internal collaboration and networking.

Introduction

As previously seen, social media has largely been positioned within the marketing department or the customer service department. And for a good number of organizations, these two key areas are where it continues to reside.

As social technologies have evolved over the years, and adoption and usage of the platforms has increased, the use of social media within organizations to aid their own internal communications has become more commonplace.

There is an increasing body of evidence, some of which we'll refer to throughout this chapter, which shows that social technologies are fast developing as an internal resource helping organizations to become more collaborative, creative and connected. The growth of these internal social networks is driving a sense of belonging and community amongst employees, and ultimately assisting with very tangible improvements in employee engagement, productivity, innovation and ultimately profitability.

In this chapter we'll explore the rise of internal social media usage for business, and how social media technologies used internally are helping organizations to break down organizational and operational silos, drive innovation, save time and enable employees and teams to collaborate more effectively.

The potential benefits

Improving the productivity and effectiveness of people within organizations has been a hot topic since business began.

At a time when we have more communication channels at our fingertips than ever before, the challenge of low productivity and employee disengagement continues to rise. According to a Gallup report, just one in ten British people feel engaged at work, and just 10 per cent of Western European workers are generally engaged, compared with 33 per cent of those in the US.[1] Even at best, those statistics illustrate that approximately, on average, 70 per cent of the workforce are not engaged.

The Gallup report, lack of engagement and low productivity can be largely attributed to unnecessary admin and poor communication:

- the average worker spends 13 hours a week on emails alone, which means 28 per cent of the working week is taken up by email management;
- 86 per cent of corporate executives, employees and educators say that ineffective communication is a big reason for failures in the workplace;
- 58 per cent say poor management is the biggest challenge getting in the way of productivity.

It's inspiring to learn, then, that a number of organizations are turning to internal social media technologies to connect employees in a far more effective way.

Former professor at Harvard Business School Thierry Breton, CEO of France-based information technology services firm Atos Origin, which has more than 70,000 employees across 40 territories, introduced an internal social network to the workplace, reducing the use of email by 60 per cent across the organization. His aim is to turn Atos into a zero-email company.[2]

The introduction of social technologies is reported to have improved the sharing of knowledge across the enterprise, making it easier to locate subject matter experts and, importantly, allow for more efficient collaboration.

McKinsey Global Institute reports a rise in productivity of workers of 20–25 per cent when using social media technologies to enhance communications, knowledge sharing and collaboration.[3]

As well as productivity, there's also the opportunity to unlock talent and knowledge within organizations to drive innovation. A research article by ACAS described an example from South Eastern Railway, who turned to social technologies to connect and communicate with its dispersed employee base of around 4,000 people.[4] They developed a bespoke social network which brought their staff together to deal with work issues, and provided a sense of 'voice' to employees so they could more easily speak out, alert others to challenges, get answers and provide solutions to others.

As appetite for internal social networks increases, so too does the range of off-the-shelf internal social network solutions. In 2018, Facebook launched Facebook Workplace for Business, a dedicated space for employees to connect, communicate and collaborate on work-related initiatives.

Building upon the widespread adoption of Facebook, all the familiar features and functionality such as Messenger, livestreaming video and trending stories are available on Workplace. The only difference between Facebook's consumer platform and the corporate platform is that an individual's accounts can't be mixed, and all the content in Facebook Workplace is owned by the employer rather than Facebook. Due to ease of adoption, it's proving to be a popular solution, and Facebook highlight over 30,000 case studies across a range of businesses, such as Volkswagen, who highlight findings that efficiency is up and emails are down.[5]

Heineken also uses Facebook's Workplace for internal collaboration, saying: 'It's very intuitive and people are already very familiar with how to use Facebook. No special instructions are required.' Royal Bank of Scotland also encourages employees to use the platform: 'It lets our staff communicate discuss and solve problems faster and more efficiently in a way that tools such as email simply can't.'

As well as the Facebook Workplace case studies, you'll find an excellent resource in Rachel Miller's evergreen blog post in which she cites over 400 internal social media use cases.[6] Rachel has curated case studies from organizations around the world, covering a range of internal social media platforms such as Microsoft Teams, including messaging and communication resources such as Skype and Slack, with others such as, Yammer, Jive, Jostle and Salesforce's Chatter.

Yet, as logical as it seems to connect employees via internal social networks to enable them to work more collaboratively, the use of internal social media is currently far from mainstream.

Going back to the ACAS research, they found that while many employers are keen to exploit social media to manage their external image and promote their products and services, far fewer are currently as keen to use it to engage with their own staff.

The challenges of internal social media

The lack of mainstream adoption may be aligned with the obvious challenges that companies face when implementing new technologies. The usual education and behavioural changes required to adopt a new way of doing things can cause friction and take considerable manpower.

There's no point in investing in the adoption of new technologies just for the sake of keeping up. Hence, it's important to have clear objectives as to what you want the internal social network to achieve, and a clear understandings of what's going to fit within the organizational context, based on current behaviours.

It's potentially worth taking a social approach at the outset, getting employees involved by canvassing opinions and including them in research of current resources, so that there is a sense of employees and organizations co-creating a solution.

The role of leadership

Another challenge relates to leadership, and the related cultural and operational shifts required to develop a more connected and collaborative workforce. Such organizational and people management elements run far deeper than simply deciding which internal social media technology to select and ensuring teams are trained effectively. These shifts need to be driven from the top of the organization – which brings us to exploring the important role leadership plays.

Roland Deiser, Director at the Center for the Future of Organization at the Drucker School of Management, in a recent podcast interview with the authors, referred to social technologies as 'hierarchy busters'.[7] To reap the benefits of internal social technologies, organizations need to develop or transform internal structures and operations to become more open, flatter and non-hierarchical and to create a culture of trust.

A recent study by Ashridge Leadership Education and Hult International Business School highlights the advantage social media offers as a tool for organizations to improve agility, interaction, content-sharing, knowledge and collaboration.[8] It also focuses on how social channels improve leadership effectiveness by enforcing clarity and transparency of communication – increasing speed, breadth and, importantly, intimacy to enhance the relationship between leaders and followers.

The Ashridge study further identifies that internal social media communication makes clarity around organizational strategy highly necessary. This point was elaborated upon in another podcast interview by the authors with the lead researcher of the Ashridge Study, Professor Patricia Hinds. She discussed how the use of social media within organizations was shining a light on the necessary clarity of organizational strategy – driving leaders and those tasked with communicating strategy and purpose throughout organizations to create consistent and clear lines of communication.

Paul Frampton Calero, ex-CEO of Havas Group, also shared with us a number of examples of how social technology was critical in keeping him connected with his employee base around the world. It not only enabled him to connect and regularly tune in to employee voice, regardless of geography, but also gave voice to those employees that he either wouldn't ordinarily get to meet or who wouldn't feel confident to speak out in a room.

Implementation – the practicalities

The blistering rate of technological advancement and digital transformation continues to impact society and organizations within that society. We've talked about the adoption rates of mainstream social networks, and so too how the tools we choose to connect and communicate externally are likely to permeate our working environments too.

After all, in just the same way as they give individuals the opportunity to tune in and reach out to anyone and share their voice outside of the organization, so too do internal social networks provide the same opportunity – not only for employees, but for leaders and CEOs too.

This together with the associated growth in importance of agility and collaboration to organizational success, as highlighted in just some of the studies we've mentioned in this chapter and throughout this book, means it's likely that internal social networks will indeed become mainstream and business-as-usual in the not too distant future.

As part of implementation, there are some practicalities to consider:

- Lead from the top. Get senior leaders on board, allowing others within the organization to engage and embrace a more social way of communicating.

- Have a clear objective as to the challenge your internal social network is looking to solve/improve – and work from that starting point. If there isn't a reason for people to use the channels, they won't.

- Research which channels your teams are familiar with and what's going to work with your organizational culture. For example, if 99 per cent of your workforce use Facebook socially, then Facebook's Workplace platform may be the perfect fit. Get your teams involved from a user research perspective, so they belong from the outset.

Engaging employees

For the employee, engagement is about being fully invested as a team member, focused on clear goals, being trusted and empowered, receiving regular and constructive feedback, developing new skills, and being thanked and recognized for achievements.

In a Queens University of Charlotte survey, 80 per cent of Millennials (aged 18-29) would prefer real-time feedback over traditional performance reviews. 89 per cent of them use social networks as communication tools in the workplace, and 40 per cent would even pay for social tools to use within the workplace to increase efficiency.[9]

Top-performing organizations are building community – fostering the sense that employees at all levels are in it together. These organizations are creating the opportunity for social interactions using the latest new media technologies. Those that do this well typically see improved productivity levels and better financial performance.

For the employer, engagement is about positive attitudes, drawing on employees' knowledge and skills for improvement, better communication, and making sure the company's values are consistent and respected.

Conclusion

While social networks such as Facebook, Twitter, Instagram, YouTube and LinkedIn were originally developed to enable people to connect and broadcast externally, the benefits have been appropriated into dedicated tools, and are being used in their native form too, to help organizations with internal collaboration and networking.

As the boundaries between the social platforms we use as part of our personal day-to-day lives and the tools and resources we use in our working lives continue to blend, it makes sense for social networking technologies to be optimized within and across organizations, creating a more natural, connected and networked culture.

Notes

1   Just one in 10 Brits feel engaged at work, says Gallup: www.
     peoplemanagement.co.uk/news/articles/one-in-10-brits-engaged-work
     (archived at https://perma.cc/8BZP-YYPW)
2   Why Atos origin is striving to be a zero-email company: www.forbes.com/
     sites/davidburkus/2016/07/12/why-atos-origin-is-striving-to-be-a-zero-email-
     company (archived at https://perma.cc/679N-HM23)
3   The social economy: Unlocking value and productivity through social
     technologies: www.mckinsey.com/industries/technology-media-and-
     telecommunications/our-insights/the-social-economy (archived at https://
     perma.cc/2UB8-M6DL)
4   Employee engagement: Decoding social media for the workplace: www.
     hrzone.com/perform/business/employee-engagement-decoding-social-media-
     for-the-workplace (archived at https://perma.cc/67SN-Y2BD)
5   Workplace case studies: www.facebook.com/workplace/case-studies (archived
     at https://perma.cc/GW3C-TY7K)
6   Who's using what for internal social media: www.allthingsic.com/list (archived
     at https://perma.cc/NWV8-R4YD)
7   The connected leader podcast: www.carvillcreative.co.uk/podcasts (archived at
     https://perma.cc/PXN4-WMC5)
8   Leadership in an age of social media: www.hrmagazine.co.uk/article-details/
     leadership-in-an-age-of-social-media (archived at https://perma.cc/C9QT-
     T9BH)
9   Communicating in the modern workplace: https://online.queens.edu/
     infographic/253/full (archived at https://perma.cc/GD4Z-3HBP)

SOCIAL MEDIA IS FULL OF #FAKENEWS

Misinformation, parody and satire exist, as they always have, in different mediums and formats. It's essential to use trusted sources, critical thinking and to be a cautious consumer of media, irrespective of the platform.

Introduction

'Fake news' made its first appearance on *Dictionary.com* in 2017, but it is hardly a novel concept. Concern about misinformation in media, and politicians and public figures disliking media coverage is nothing new. Consider the American President who said, 'There has been more new error propagated by the press in the last ten years than in a hundred years before.' That was John Adams, in 1798.[1]

Although fake news and misinformation may be widespread on social media, it is hard to know whether it is any different, or more pernicious, to before. Research by Lazer and colleagues in 2018, published in *Science*, suggested that there is still limited understanding and research around the scale and effect of fake news.[2] They suggest that rigorous research still needs to be conducted to understand how much fake news is out there, what effects it really has on people, and how individuals and social media platforms filter information.

> *Fake news:* false news stories, often of a sensational nature, created to be widely shared or distributed for the purpose of generating revenue, or promoting or discrediting a public figure, political movement, company, etc.

The accusation that information on social media can be distorted, biased or massaged is certainly true. Similar accusations have been hurled at newspapers, books, pamphlets and any other medium used for communicating information. In 17th-century Britain, King Charles II issued 'A Proclamation to restrain the Spreading of False News', meaning information that the king worried was helping 'to nourish an universal jealousy and dissatisfaction in the minds of all His Majesties good subjects'. It stopped short of complaining about Crooked Cromwell – very unfair!

Different types of fake news

When looking at the veracity of news and information on social media, you'll probably notice that there are grey areas. This is how we categorize and define how we see these: there are truths that can be objectively proved; there are statements that are true for a particular person; there are outright falsehoods; then there are exaggerated lies. For example:

1 Ben Nevis is the tallest mountain in the UK.

2 Mount Snowdon is the tallest mountain I've ever seen in the UK!

3 Mount Snowdon is huge; it must be the biggest in the UK.

4 Mount Snowdon is the tallest mountain in the world!

The first is objectively true and easily verifiable. The second could certainly be accurate for one person or many people. Then, it's a slippery slope down to the third and fourth statements. But it is incredibly useful to distinguish between objective facts, people's observations, and blatant lies.

Tandoc, Lim and Ling conducted some very useful research on news and fake news.[3] They identify different types of 'fake' news which vary widely in purpose, context, audience. The first three types are satire, parody and fabrication, and we're going to discuss these in detail now because those are more closely aligned with common usages of the term 'fake news'. We'll cover the final three types, photo manipulation, PR and propaganda, more briefly, because they are a bit further from the common usage.

News satire

News satire is one of the most common types of 'fake news' in the research literature. This uses a humorous and often exaggerated approach, presenting information in the format of a typical news broadcast. There are plenty of examples of these with a long history, with shows such as *Mock the Week* and *Have I Got News For You* in the UK and *Saturday Night Live's Weekend Update* and the *Late Show with Stephen Colbert* in the US. Satire presents news that is deliberately distorted for comedic purposes. It often presents stories that sound as if they could be true, but are not.

However, there is a trend towards satire becoming a staple of mainstream media as a method of presenting criticism, shaping political opinions and affecting discourse, and this inevitably filters through to social media. This is not a completely new idea: the ancient Greeks wrote plays that satirized the forms of government of the neighbouring city-states, and in 1729 Jonathan Swift's *A Modest Proposal* satirically (and elaborately) explained how the solution to famine in Ireland was to eat babies. Satire is often an effective form of rhetoric that resonates with people.

News fabrication

News fabrication is a style of manufacturing false information but presenting it as truth. This is more pernicious because it is deliberately designed to misrepresent facts and to misinform the audience. The format is fundamentally different from parody and satire because of the relationship between the presenter of the information and the reader or viewer. In the comedic presentation of parody or satire, there is an understanding that the consumer is not meant to take the information entirely seriously.

In their article, Tandoc and colleagues go on to explain that news fabrication makes use of partial truths, deliberately misinterpreting facts and drawing an audience biases to create a narrative that is presented as factual. These often have a political bias from either side of the political spectrum, for example the right-wing site Breitbart, or on the left The Canary. Often news fabrication combines a variety of factual (or at least plausible) sources of information to manufacture misinformation. Some of these sites mix 'fake' news with plausible or verifiable stories – so although certain sources can sometimes be a reliable source of information, they need to be treated very skeptically.

News parody

News parody is another humorous interpretation of a mainstream news format, but it often deliberately uses false information for comedic effect. This format has flourished online with many publications like The Onion or The Beaverton, which present fake stories in a new format that are intended to be deliberately outrageous or surprising. The intention behind this type of information is intended to be delivered as a sly wink. The information is presented seriously, but the reader is supposed to know that the content is completely fabricated for comedic purposes.

The distinction between news parody and news fabrication or the spread of fake news is not always clear-cut. These satirical stories have a tendency to get picked up by more legitimate news sources when writers don't check their facts or sources. The effect of this is that the lines of parody and satire can start to blur, such as when news parody website World Daily News Report reported that drag queen RuPaul had been groped by Donald Trump in the 1990s. The story was completely fabricated, but quickly spread across tabloids and social media.

The next three categories are more familiar ways of massaging the truth or distorting information.

Photo manipulation

This is a way of misrepresenting visual instead of written information. It is common practice, and widely recognized, that images are often touched up, changed, edited or modified from the original. Photo manipulation has become more common in relation to news fabrication. For example, images can be combined, modified and edited to include a logo from a news website to fabricate images that are presented as real.

Advertising and PR

In the context of fake news, this describes promotional material passed off as news for financial gain. This occurs when advertising is presented as a news report, or a press release is published as news. The distortion is 'when public relations practitioners adopt the practices and/or appearance of journalists in order to insert marketing or other persuasive messages into news media'.[4]

These is very prevalent online – paid marketing content which does not give any indication to the reader that it is actually an advertisement.

Propaganda

Propaganda is not new, but there has been a re-emergence of interest in information that is distorted for political purposes. These stories are usually misrepresentations of facts, presented as news but designed to benefit a political leader, group or organization. For example, research on Channel One in Russia shows long-term patterns of a media company that presents itself as news, but is used to distribute 'strategic narratives' and shape political narratives, with little regard to facts or evidence.

The final definition of fake news is an interesting appropriation of the term that can be credited to Donald Trump. In a 2018 tweet, Trump said: '91% of the network news about me is Negative (fake)'.[5]

This idea of 'fake news' as used by the US President does not fit neatly into any of the first six categories. The content of the statement is rather revealing about this particular use of the term. Instead of referring to the veracity of information, in this context it refers to the relationship between the information and its subject. 'Fake' here means undesirable. Any news that does not shine a positive light on its subject is dismissed as 'fake news' (the meaning conflates unfavourable and untrue).

Donald Trump's lawyer Rudy Giuliani explained this approach with the phrase 'Truth isn't truth' – meaning: this is the world as I'd like to see it, irrespective of facts. It's ultimately an issue of clearly differentiating facts from opinions.[6] Both facts and opinions can be genuine and legitimate, but must be clearly separated. Good news sources do this by clearly separating news from editorial. The line on social media is often more blurred, so the responsibility falls upon the reader to distinguish between facts, fabrication and opinion.

The challenge for business

Good, successful businesses operate on accurate information. Any business needs to understand their people and performance. Information about the market and competitors is essential for operating successfully. Knowledge about laws and regulations are necessary to maintain and run a business. Accurate information about customers and clients is vital for a company to provide goods or services.

Effective decision-making in business relies on using good information. Economic and labour market forecasts, consumer demand, market research and regulatory environments will all affect business performance. The decisions made by leaders of teams, departments and companies will rely on the most accurate information and the best available projections.

Let's use the example of a company looking for a new location to build a call centre in the UK. The company needs a relatively large, mobile workforce who can be trained relatively quickly and develop further skills while working

There are two potential sources of information about the number of workers available in the chosen location. Firstly, there is a former factory owner turned local politician who campaigned on reducing unemployment. This politician runs a social media account that posts publicity photos in factories, alongside photos of empty job centres. The running theme from their social media is that unemployment has been drastically reduced in the area. Secondly, government numbers from the Office of National Statistics (ONS) show relatively high unemployment in the area, which suggests there are many people looking for work.

Let's assume that both are relatively accurate in their portrayal. The first shows genuine photos that show people working and empty job centres. The second represents accurate numbers for the overall proportion of people who are unemployed in the area. Who is to be believed? Which is the best source of information for a business?

There isn't necessarily a clear-cut answer here. Large, national representative research conducted by a reliable organization with rigorous research methods like the ONS tends to be the most consistently reliable. As a general rule, numbers from the ONS would be much more reliable for making an initial assessment.

But effective business intelligence should consider both sources of information and thoughtfully weigh the credibility of each. Social media may be a good start in reaching out to people in the area for more information and contacts. Initial research may lead to a visit to that area. Chat to taxi drivers about how business is in the area, check out the local shops and job centres, talk to the Chambers of Commerce, leading business and industry association. Social media is a great way of assessing opinions, but it is supplementary to, not a replacement for, first-hand research.

Potential problems of fake news for organizations

Operating on the assumption of fake news

Fake news has the potential to damage businesses directly by spreading misinformation about the business, or people within it, or the way it operates. It should not be automatically assumed that news or information on social media is untrue, but the lack of any editorial control or curation means information on social media must be approached with a level of scepticism.

Fake news can also create significant problems if it is used as the primary source of information in business planning. Distorted economic data, labour market information or misrepresentations of public opinion are readily available. If business plans are built on incorrect data, the effects are likely to be disappointing at best, and catastrophic at worst.

Using and spreading fake news (outputs)

There is significant and long-lasting reputational damage from being affiliated with fake news. Many PR departments are familiar with a bit of PR spin, but deliberately distorting or manipulating data is not just a PR risk, it is fraud.

We don't have to look far to see the damage that has been done to people and businesses when they deliberately lie. It destroyed Enron nearly two decades ago, and was one of the many issues in the now infamous failure that was the Fyre Festival in 2017. One of the most clear and consistent findings on fake news is that although it can spread rapidly, it tends to diffuse much more quickly than information that is accurate.

Evaluating information

Susan Nolan writes about evaluating fake news for the American Psychological Association.[7] One simple and effective method for evaluating the veracity of information is a framework with a pleasing acronym: the CRAAP test.[8]

This uses five categories to evaluate information and its source. Each category comes with some questions the reader should consider about the source to assess its trustworthiness:

1 **Currency**: the timeliness of the information. Is it recent, and has it been updated? Is there more recent information available, or will older sources work as well?

2 **Relevance**: how important the information is for you. Is it sufficiently simple or advanced for your requirements? Have you looked at other sources to see if it is relevant to you? Would you be comfortable relying on this source of information?

3 **Authority**: the source of the information. Is it reliable? Can you tell who published the information? Is it from a real person or organization? Is there contact information, or is it anonymous?

4 **Accuracy**: the reliability of the information. Is it supported by good evidence? Any evidence? Can the information be verified using another reliable source? Does the language seem unbiased and free from errors?

5 **Purpose**: the reason for the information existing. What is the purpose of the information? Does it intend to argue, teach, sell, entertain, persuade or call to action? Is the purpose clear? Is it fact, opinion, advertising or propaganda?

Strong, healthy businesses run on facts, good research and credible information. Business decisions need to be made based on evidence. Businesses should be particularly careful about evaluating information that is to be used in decision-making or planning. We talk about the particulars of using social media in business and advertising in detail in Chapter 10.

Conclusion

Misinformation, parody and satire exist, as they always have, in different mediums and formats. It's essential to use trusted sources, critical thinking and to be a cautious consumer of media, irrespective of the platform.

It is equally important for businesses and those within them to be responsible consumers of information when preparing company reports, financial statements, press reports and internal documents. Relying on inaccurate information leads to poor judgement and poor decision-making. The ability to evaluate what is good evidence brings competitive advantage for businesses.

Notes

1   The age-old problem of 'Fake News': www.smithsonianmag.com/history/
    age-old-problem-fake-news-180968945 (archived at https://perma.cc/EZL6-
    3LRY)

2   Lazer, D M et al (2018) The science of fake news, *Science*, 359 (**6380**),
    pp 1094–96

3   Tandoc, E C, Lim, Z W and Ling, R (2018) Defining 'Fake News': A typology
    of scholarly definitions, *Digital Journalism*, 6 (**2**), pp 137–53

4   Fake news TV: Widespread and undisclosed: www.prwatch.org/fakenews/
    execsummary (archived at https://perma.cc/8PPD-QPF8)

5   Retrieved from https://twitter.com/realDonaldTrump/
    status/994179864436596736 (archived at https://perma.cc/7FJ5-ZVUJ)

6   Trump lawyer Rudy Giuliani: Truth isn't truth: www.bbc.co.uk/news/world-
    us-canada-45241838 (archived at https://perma.cc/3TZN-JUXJ)

7   Critical thinking and information fluency: Fake news in the classroom:
    www.apa.org/ed/precollege/ptn/2017/05/fake-news (archived at https://perma.
    cc/SUK7-GEVV)

8   Blakeslee, S (2004) The CRAAP test, *LOEX Quarterly*, 31 (**3**), pp 6–7

IT'S NOT WORTH RESPONDING TO CRITICISM ON SOCIAL MEDIA

It can take a bit of work to sort the troublemakers from the legitimate complaints. But responding to complaints and criticism on social media is well worth the effort when it is done well.

Introduction

One of the risks for any business active on social media is that not all your interactions will necessarily be positive. Even the best businesses will sometimes make mistakes, and even the most well-intentioned organizations may come up against people with intentions that are not entirely constructive.

Avoiding social media does not free companies from criticism online. People will take to social media to complain about businesses they dislike or take grievance with, even if the organization is not on social media. The advantage of participating in social media activity is that you can take more active steps to manage your reputation online and be more responsive to people.

We also shouldn't necessarily take criticism as a negative thing. Many people who have a complaint or a criticism actually have a resolution in mind. In psychological terms, 'frustration' is the negative emotional response when a goal is blocked or denied. Often when a customer or a client can't get their legitimate and relevant problem solved by the business in a traditional setting such as in-person or over the phone, they will take to social media. If there is a solution to be had, this is a good opportunity for the organization to recognize, address, and solve the problem. Most people will actually be quite satisfied if you acknowledge the problem and help them fix it.

Of course, not everyone has the best intentions online. A small minority of people do just like to cause chaos, harass people or companies and stir up trouble. This means it can take a bit of work to sort the troublemakers from the legitimate complaints. But responding to complaints and criticism on social media is well worth the effort when it is done well.

Response times

Social media is a fast-moving communication platform. For better or worse, many people will be quick to take to social media, sometimes even narrating their problem or complaint in real time. As discussed in Chapter 12, your business does not necessarily need to be online 24/7, but you should have target response times for interactions on social media.

Responding quickly and diffusing tensions can help to keep the problem from escalating and shows the person that you are listening and taking them seriously. Also pay careful attention to what the person is saying in their first post. If they are asking for something clear and concrete, it should make the response fairly straightforward. If their product was faulty, there should be some clear steps to rectifying the problem. If they had a poor customer service experience, perhaps an apology is in order. The first thing you should try to identify is what their desired outcome is (or was). Complaints, in general, should be relatively straightforward to resolve in a satisfactory way if you know what the other person wants to get out of the interaction.

If you cannot figure out what the person who is complaining actually wants, or they will not tell you, perhaps there is nothing more that can be offered than an apology. For any lengthier interaction, it may be better to have the discussion in private or direct messages instead of a more public forum.

Public vs private responses

Not all public complaints require a public response, and public forums are not always the best place to solve complex problems. If a quick and easy fix or a simple apology is all that is required, then a public response may be a good option. If the problem cannot be solved in 280 characters, a private conversation may be a much better approach.

In many cases, people also take to social media for response when they cannot get through to a real person. Some companies deliberately set up convoluted and automated messaging services to prevent customers talking with a real person at the business. Some tech companies such as Facebook and Uber make it almost impossible to talk to a real person, and Her Majesty's Revenue and Customs' phone contact information has a convoluted labyrinth of options to select, almost everyone one of which ends at the same point: the caller is advised to check the website shortly before the phone line disconnects.

This often results in frustration, and some people will choose to take to social media after their other options for making a complaint or venting their frustrations are thwarted. So unless your business model involves deliberately blocking people from contacting you, a good solution could be to offer a direct message, email or phone contact to the person who has a complaint.

Offering to discuss the problem privately can prevent some of the problems that public communication on social media has the potential to amplify. Complaints on a public forum can sometimes turn into grandstanding. In public confrontations, both sides are more likely to try and save face or be seen as the winner of a conflict, and this can be counterproductive when trying to come to a resolution. It can be easier for both sides to de-escalate conflict, work to solve a complex problem and come to a satisfactory resolution without bystanders and spectators.

Do not escalate

For many people, the natural response to complaints or criticism is to defend. Perhaps it was a complete oversight despite the best intentions of people in the company. Sometimes it is a problem that was completely outside of the organization's control. Maybe the criticism is a bit too aggressively directed at people who genuinely want to help. Sometimes people and organizations are hesitant to admit any fault, worrying that it could compound the problems.

In most cases, though, an apology and a promise to resolve the issue goes a long way towards solving the problem. When possible and reasonable, the apology should offer a remedy to the problem or concrete steps towards a resolution.

Of course, anyone who has worked in customer service (these authors included) know that some people have complaints that the business cannot solve. Some people come in looking for a fight that has nothing to do with their target. A few people have other things going on in their lives, and end up making an innocent bystander the target of their own troubled mind. This cannot be avoided, but if there is clearly no resolution to the problem then avoid making the situation worse, de-escalate as much as feasible or reasonable and quietly allow the person to move along. Online, we would say *don't feed the trolls*.

If the claims are inaccurate or deliberately mischievous, it may be necessary to correct the information, and provide facts supporting your message. This must be done in a polite way, although it may be tempting to clap back with an equally sarcastic or snarky tone. But when both sides persist in lowering the tone of the discussion on social media, the whole affair can descend into madness very quickly. If you take the bait, it just fuels more activity and may even signal to others that you will engage in behaviour where no one escapes looking good.

Return to the initial point of trying to figure out what people's desired outcomes are when they make complaints online.

Actions follow words

Promises are easy to make, but it's very important that reasonable steps are taken to follow through on what people are told on social media. If the promise is to fix, or investigate, the problem then those promises must be put into action.

If the issues is complex or will take some time to solve, keep people updated on the progress. Even if the problem cannot be solved in a way that will completely satisfy the complainant, they should still see that you have taken all reasonable steps to fix the problem, or at least to figure out what went wrong and explain it to them.

A quick response and an apology may help in the short term, but it will not help if the necessary action is not taken to address the issue.

Remember your customer base

We've said that it is important to identify people's objectives when they make a complaint on social media, as well as highlighting that a small minority of people just want to cause chaos instead of having constructive intentions.

It can also be useful to consider your overall customer or client base when responding to criticism. We've discussed extensively the importance of specific messages, targeting markets and having a clearly defined approach to social media (see Chapters 10 and 12). Remember that your general approach to social media and how you interact with people online shouldn't break your focus on your core audience.

A furore can quickly break out on social media and sweep up many in its path. At times, the immediacy of social media can make problems seem far more serious than they actually are. Keep this in mind if you end up in the firing line of a social media mob who have nothing to do with your business.

While it is important to apologize for mistakes and acknowledge and resolve legitimate complaints, be more cautious about getting mixed up in a controversy that is not directly related to your organization or its stakeholders. If a group are unhappy with your organization, but have no relationship with you and are never likely to be customers, then their criticisms can be taken with a very large grain of salt.

It's not possible to make everyone happy on social media, so make sure you don't throw your own customers or employees under the bus to appease virtual pitchfork-wielding mobs.

Employee guidelines

We discussed employee guidelines for social media in Chapter 8. There is no need to restate them in great detail, but your guidelines explain how to interact with complainants on the organization's social media account or when acting on behalf of the organization.

Guidelines for staff who manage social media accounts should also include what types of behaviour on social media are unacceptable. Although much of this chapter has focused on customer complaints and resolving customer problems, it is very important to remember the well-being of the public-facing employees who deal with these complaints. While legitimate criticisms and genuine complaints may not always be expressed in the most civilized manner, abuse, harassment, or discrimination against staff must not be tolerated.

Resolute red lines for customer behaviour should be drawn for two reasons. Firstly, as stated, staff should not be subject to abuse or harassment. Secondly, this type of customer behaviour should not be rewarded in any way, as this is likely to compound the problem. For these types of cases, responsibility should be passed upward for a supervisor or manager to deal with the problem.

Conclusion

People will take their concerns and complaints online, whether or not the object of their criticism has available social channels. Organizations can use this as an opportunity to react to complaints and criticisms online, and when they do it well it will improve the overall customer service experience.

Of course, not all criticism online is constructive. It is necessary to identify which problems can be resolved, and which cannot. The approach should be clearly aligned with the company's overall objectives and communications strategy. Just remember to set the tone and communicate with people in a respectful way that aligns with your overall communications style and strategy.

SOCIAL MEDIA IS FOR POSTING PICTURES OF YOUR BREAKFAST

*It's all about getting the right message on the right channels.
If you're in the restaurant business, posting photos
of the restaurant's food may be exactly the right
social media strategy.*

Introduction

It's a common sight on social media: people's photos of their breakfast or lunch, photos of pets, animals or popular tourist destinations. This is one of the frequent criticisms of social media use. Some journalists seem to relish going after people's personal use of social media, like the *New York Times'* amusing 'The tyranny of other people's vacation photos', or an article in *Vice* entitled 'How Instagram makes you basic, boring, and completely deranged'.[1,2] But these articles tell you a great deal more about the author than their subject matter.

The advantage (and the disadvantage) of social media is that the content is what you choose to make it. Some people will tell you it is a great way to connect with people; others will say social media is full of conflict and vitriol. Both may be right, and the reason is because you engineer your own social circle, discussion topics, advertising environment and discourse on social media.

Often, businesses will question whether they want to be part of social media when they do not realize there is no single, monolithic, social media environment. For businesses, participating in social media is not about engaging with every person, on every level, in every location about any and all topics. A little bit of focus and purpose goes a very long way.

The advantage that comes with social media is that it allows a person or a business to post and publish exactly what they want. Users and communities form around specific topics. Many of these groups share photos, stories and comments about everyday life. Although this is commonplace, it does not mean a business is required to get involved in any or all of these discussions.

The advantage of social media forming around specific topics, communities and areas of interest means it allows the users to tailor their approach and content specifically to certain communities and interest groups. Of course, this does tend to create filter bubbles, but this is not always negative (as we discuss in Chapter 28).

Focus on the right audience

As we will see in a case study later in this chapter, social media is most effective when you are using it with a clear message and purpose in mind, and have decided on a style and approach to your messaging. If someone shows up to give a press conference completely unprepared, what they end up saying could end up being surprising and confusing to their audience as well as the presenter. Choose the content, the purpose and shape the message first, then choose the channels and style which fits.

This is where social media for personal use sharply diverges from business use. Many people choose to have individual social media pages to share, discuss and post about whatever they want. Businesses would be unwise to take the same approach with their social channels.

This doesn't mean that business-related social media activity cannot be spontaneous, informal, fun, personal, or even a bit unpredictable. But for businesses, the social media activity should fit within a framework of the what the company does, who they are, what they are trying to communicate, and with whom they are communicating.

This typically includes some level of customer profiling, where you discover certain characteristics of your customers, including:

- **Demographic factors**: different aspects about people's background like gender, age, occupation, marital status or family composition.

- **Geographic factors**: where people live or where they are visiting. For businesses with a physical location, the customers are usually geographically close to a physical location, and it's important not to forget this when targeting people online.

- **Psychological factors**: people's motivation, personality, values, and other factors that can vary substantially between people and explain individual decision-making.

- **Economic factors**: differences in income, occupation, and spending patterns.

Finding the right channels

Once you know who your customer is (or have defined what characteristics your customers have, you get a better sense of who they are and why they might be interested in your business. Then it's much more straightforward to understand which social channels they are using, and what might appeal to them on those channels.

Social media often gets criticism for people posting photos of their meals or similar activities that not everyone is interested in. If you're a major law firm, or a car manufacturer, pictures of employee breakfasts may not be the ideal content. However, if you've got an excellent subsidized staff restaurant, and you're advertising perks for employees as part of a recruitment programme, that may be one of the best things to post. It can still be useful to distinguish these channels. Some companies choose to delineate these with a 'Jobs at this Company' page, which is separate from the page discussing their products or services.

It's all about getting the right message on the right channels. If you're in the restaurant business, posting photos of the restaurant's food may be exactly the right social media strategy, as we explain in the example below.

Best practice example – Tonkotsu

To get some additional insight into specific examples of best practice and professional insight on social media, we spoke to Ashleigh Muir, Brand Manager at Tonkotsu.

Tonkotsu is a ramen restaurant with locations in Birmingham and London. It started up its first location in London in 2012, enjoyed great success and grew quickly to 10 locations. As of 2019, they've secured additional investment funding to open further locations.[3]

It's also worth noting that their food works very well in a visual medium. Food reviewers love a sensual description, so it's best to use their words: 'And then the deep, luscious Tonkotsu ramen arrived filled with silky noodles, slices of soft pork belly, half a seasoned soft-boiled egg and with a slick of black garlic oil across the top.'[4] But times are moving on, and getting good photos of great looking food online can be even more effective than a delectable review in the *Times* or the *Guardian*.

Their social media activity is certainly proving to be effective, making excellent use of the visual medium to showcase their food. We initially heard of Tonkotsu through recommendations from others who had discovered it on their social media pages. The pictures of the food on their social channels are certainly appealing – more than appealing enough to attract one of the authors to visit the restaurant in the interests of conducting field research.

Interview

Ashleigh Muir, Tonkotsu's Brand Manager, estimates that about 40 per cent of Tonkotsu's new customers discover them first on social media. She said it can be challenging to estimate exactly how many people visit the restaurant as a direct result of discovering them on social channels. But on channels like Instagram, they get a very good sense of the interest online, and analytics tools are useful for understanding how many people engage with their posts and share them with others. And of course, when the food looks great people want to come in and share photos of their meals.

Muir describes Tonkotsu's overall approach to their social media presence as 'informative, but fairly relaxed'. They use it to share images of the restaurant, the food and people enjoying themselves restaurant without using more aggressive marketing tactics. A combination of more relaxed and fun photos, and great food at the physical locations, helps the food to sell itself.

'We tend to use it as a tool to share great imagery of our fantastic food, and for connecting with our followers in a fun way, instead of heavily advertising with lots of calls to action and 'click this and do that'-type advertising,' Muir says.

Muir says their social media has always been handled internally. Initially the founders managed the social channels, but as the company grew and Muir joined the company as brand manager, she took over the accounts. She has sole responsibility for the company's social media activity, saying she may decide to share this with other employees in future, but plans to always keep it internal.

She describes how their social media activity has changed both with the growth of the company and the rise of social media. 'We've always used social media, but we rely on it a lot more these days than when we did back in 2012.

For us, social media is the quickest and most efficient way to share news and information with our followers and potential new customers.'

Muir talks about how she and the business have seen social media evolve, and how she thinks video-based channels are likely to become even more influential. 'Video seems to be the next big thing, with apps like TikTok and Lasso becoming very popular,' she says. What's more, businesses need to understand these trends, and be open to using new platforms, switching and sometimes leaving old platforms behind. 'Using the same platforms as your target customer is always important to stay relevant, so there may be a platform we pick up or leave behind in future.'

Muir also talks about the targets and metrics they use to measure engagement and activity. She says they don't set hard targets related to social media, but do have goals related to their online following and engagement; however: 'everything is done organically'. This connects nicely with their general approach to social media, with a more relaxed and fun (but still business-savvy) approach.

It also leads nicely into the advice Muir has for new businesses starting out on social media: 'Don't fall into the trap of paying people to get you new followers'. She advises a slower, deliberate and more strategic approach – get more people interested in your business as it grows, have a great product, and post about it on social. 'Growing your following and engagement is best done organically, by posting great imagery with engaging captions. It's not worth getting your account shut down over! Slow and steady wins the race.'

When I asked her what she likes to see from their customers on social media, Muir said, 'We love it when customers share snaps of their food, or of them enjoying their time in our restaurants. We quite often repost them and share them with our own followers. We also welcome any feedback (positive or negative) through any of our social channels. We want to be easily contactable by whatever way is best for our customers.'

Strategy summary

Here are a few of the key points summarizing Tonkotsu's social media strategy:

- accounts are internally managed
- a focus on visually-oriented posts (ideal for Instagram), showing visually appealing products
- emphasis on organic growth and not on paid marketing
- a fun, informal style
- a post frequency of about five times per week
- encouraging customers to upload and share photos

Conclusion

There are useful lessons to learn here about how any company builds a cohesive and attractive presence on social media. However, it's not very helpful or constructive to give advice about what specifically social media should be 'for', or exactly what type of content succeeds.

Social media is a collection of different communication platforms, so the question for a business is precisely what message they are looking to send, and to whom. Like any business activity, the company's social media approach has to align with the business' own strategy and targets – unfortunately there is no magic bullet or one-size-fits-all approach.

Posting photos of food on social media is not for everyone – but it certainly is a good business strategy for a restaurant.

Notes

1   The tyranny of other people's vacation photos: www.nytimes.com/2016/08/14/ fashion/vacation-photos-facebook-instagram.html (archived at https://perma. cc/WWD5-7UC7)

2   How Instagram makes you basic, boring, and completely deranged: www.vice. com/en_us/article/vbbjbx/how-instagram-makes-you-basic-boring-and-completely-deranged (archived at https://perma.cc/ZF3A-6PHU)

3   Ramen chain Tonkotsu eyes expansion with YFM backing: www.cityam.com/ ramen-chain-tonkotsu-eyes-expansion-with-yfm-backing (archived at https:// perma.cc/B2QK-MHPY)

4   Restaurant review: Tonkotsu, London: www.theguardian.com/ lifeandstyle/2012/nov/25/tonkotsu-restaurant-review-jay-rayner (archived at https://perma.cc/AU8V-3JQ9)

MYTH 17

OVERSHARING ON SOCIAL MEDIA CAN REVEAL TRADE SECRETS

*Data security, trade secrets and goodwill are key
to organizational success. It's important that provisions
are in place to protect the organization, and that
employees are clear on their responsibilities.*

Introduction

Social networks and technologies such as blogs, forums and other networked platforms have become powerful in connecting organizations with customers and, as explored in Chapter 13, increasingly in connecting businesses with their own employees.

With more than 50 per cent of the world engaged on social networks, they have increasingly become business as usual, and for a business to totally remove them from mainstream business activity could potentially put that business at a disadvantage, trailing behind their competitors.

However, given that social media communication is generally far freer and more casual, there's good reason why the cautious are concerned about the challenge and risk of oversharing on social media. Such informality can lead to unintentionally revealing trade secrets for all and sundry, including competitors, to see.

Empowering the use of social media within organizations and advising employees to be careful about what they share sounds, on the face of it, pretty simple. Provide a clear framework within which to operate, share the organizational guidelines across the organization, provide clarity on the dos and don'ts, ensure everything is updated in the employee handbook – and job done.

But in just the same way that being 'social' is deeply ingrained within the complexities of how we communicate, so too are there complexities in managing the risks associated with this less formal means of communication.

While we're both advocates and champions of social media for business, it would be remiss of us to exclude a chapter on the risks that organizations need to safeguard against when it comes to engaging with social media. Therefore, in this chapter we'll explore the risk of oversharing, take a look at some communication frameworks and social media guidelines that while, simple, engender trust – explore some of the recent legal positioning and share insights about what organizations are doing at a very practical level to mitigate risk.

Start with the end in mind

Because social media activity is so pervasive in our everyday lives, the lines around professional and personal viewpoints, and who is saying what and in what context, can easily become blurred. Of course, the whole idea of social media is to encourage sharing. That habit becomes part of natural behaviour – and yet it may be risky or sensitive for employees to talk freely about a new product they are working on, or a new client that they've just landed.

This clearly demonstrates not only that training is required when organizations embrace social media, but also that businesses need to carefully think through how business processes and job roles are to be supported or facilitated by social media.

Embracing the opportunities that come with using social media for professional networking, while at the same time safeguarding against any major risks, is something that needs to be considered end-to-end and communicated to employees, ideally in a way that is easily accessible, transparent and clear.

For example, take the role of a business development manager. It is highly likely that they will be encouraged to use their own personal social networks to enhance the work they do within the organization. Therefore, it's important to consider what the lines of control and ownership are around the use of personal social networks – including consideration around what happens when employees leave.

As well as ensuring there is clarity on that aspect, this also raises the question of who owns the social media accounts, and the case of the US sports journalist Andy Bitter. In 2018, Andy was sued by his former employer for refusing to turn over the login and password for his Twitter account when he left. While the employee handbook advised that he was obligated to turn over all company property, the Twitter account was in his personal name, and as witnessed in the tweets from his outraged followers, they considered themselves to be following him rather than the company.

What followed was a complicated legal battle, and one where Andy Bitter ended up suing the employer for defamation, which ended in a settlement. With clarity, education and clear expectation from the outset, a costly scenario could have been more amicably resolved.

Keeping employees up to speed

In 2018 we interviewed Kevin Burrowes, Managing Partner, Clients and Markets at PwC.[1] In that interview, he suggested PwC should invest in social media training for all employees, with annual exams. Employees have to pass those exams, and there are clear sanctions when guidelines they've been educated about aren't adhered to.

This provides an excellent example of employers taking responsibility to not only train and educate employees in what's expected, but also to revisit regularly to ensure everyone is up to speed – bringing clarity through continuous education as to what is and isn't permissible across the organization.

In 2020, when this book is published, we're likely to be hard-pushed to find an organization that doesn't have some form of social media guidelines in their employee handbook. However, making the assumption that employees have read the guidelines and are clear on the boundaries, organizational expectation and preferences is something that realistically needs to be checked regularly. It's equally wise to sense-check the manner in which the guidelines are being communicated, too. It's highly unlikely that employees will read and adhere to a complicated, legalese-riddled 38-page document created by a compliance team.

When it comes to social media guidelines, we particularly like the empowered positioning of the ones from Best Buy.[2] The guidelines, entitled 'Be Smart, Be Respectful, Be Human', not only speak to employees as grown-ups, enabling them to use their best judgement, but are very clear and succinct. In fact, they fit onto one highly informative page.

Ensuring data security

Whether or not an employee is properly trained on your social media guidelines, the evolution of technology, particularly around the portability of digital devices, the growth of flexible working and BYOD (bring your own device to work) schemes, data storage and connections with customers or suppliers on social media pose security and risk challenges. And when it comes to trade secrets, what seems like a genuinely innocent conversation on social media could lead to employees disclosing confidential customer data without them even realizing they are doing so.

The laws around data security are hugely complex, and differ dependent upon where you are in the world and jurisdictions.[3] That said, while issues related to social media privacy in the workplace are likely to continue, there are some highly practical things employers can be doing to engage and educate employees to safeguard data and trade secrets – striking a balance and empowering employees to converse, share and network within a clear framework of what is and isn't permissible.

It's a case of assessing where you are now as regards risk and education, and developing a process of communication to get all employees on the same page.

Some practical questions for analysis:

- Have you set clear expectations? Is there a social media mission statement that articulates clearly how social media is expected to be used within the business and how it aligns with overall business strategy and the role each employee plays?

- Do all employees take social media training? If so, how often is it revisited, and how do you know they've absorbed the key learnings – for example, are there exams?

- Do you have clear social media guidelines that are easy to locate and simple to understand – clearly detailing the dos and don'ts (in just the same way you may have user-friendly brand guidelines)?

- Are access/login and publishing rights on social media limited to relevant people?

- Do you have resource dedicated to managing and assessing the continuous changes happening within social media to ensure these are communicated swiftly and effectively across the organization?

- Is there a process for onboarding new team members so that they are trained and instantly up to speed with the social media guidelines, expectations and dos and don'ts?

- Is there a policy clearly outlining the process for handing over social media account access when an employee leaves?

These questions are by no means prescriptive – our intention is rather to provoke your thinking in this area and to provide a very simple baseline from which you can sense-check the practicality of your own guidelines and practice.

Conclusion

Social media sits within employees' work lives and personal lives, and cultivating a social media presence within an organization is increasingly an explicit part of many employees' jobs.

From a human perspective, common sense should reign supreme when educating employees and clearly communicating what's expected of them. That said, data security, trade secrets and goodwill are key to organizational success. It's important that provisions are in place to protect the organization, and that employees are clear on their responsibilities and the sanctions that could be enforced if that expected standard is not met.

We'll close with this fitting quote:

'You can no longer abstain from social media, but before you dive in head first, make sure you have addressed reputational, privacy and security concerns. Technology failure, leaked intellectual property or poor customer response times can all lead to long-term brand damage.' – Selim Ahmed, Digital Consulting, PwC

Notes

1   Carvill, M (2018) *Get Social – Social media strategy and tactics*, Kogan Page, London
2   Best buy social media policy: https://forums.bestbuy.com/t5/Welcome-News/Best-Buy-Social-Media-Policy/td-p/20492 (archived at https://perma.cc/F9T4-9ZUE)
3   How social media, technology and privacy laws are changing the landscape: www.skadden.com/insights/publications/2019/04/quarterly-insights/how-social-media-technology-and-privacy-laws (archived at https://perma.cc/8TRR-YT3X)

PEOPLE ON SOCIAL MEDIA WILL APPRECIATE MY TIPSY HUMOUR

All companies should have a social media policy that covers social media conduct in the workplace, and describes what kind of online behaviours could cause problems for the company outside it.

Introduction

Most people wouldn't show up to a board meeting, sales pitch or press conference drunk. So why do so many people seem to decide that after having a few beers, it's a good idea to get on social media and talk politics? Could it be that alcohol impairs judgement?

Social media is instantly accessible anywhere, so there are fewer barriers. When the inhibitions are down and it's so easy to jump on Twitter on a phone, many people find the draw to post on social media is impossible to resist. Alcohol is often used as a social lubricant, and social media is certainly a social activity. So why not mix the two?

Adults can make their own decisions about what they do on social media, and their intoxication levels at the time, but the more serious gaffes, faux-pas and blunders happen when the workplace is thrown into the mix.

Your brain on alcohol

Your brain is a complex decision-making organ that is constantly weighing a variety of options, judging the pros and the cons of different actions and making judgements based on previous experience and expected outcomes. When you put increasing levels of alcohol into the blood that is flowing through your brain, it slows down the activity in the prefrontal cortex. That's the area of the brain responsible for complex decision-making.[1] That means that after a couple of drinks, you're not as good at gauging the outcomes of your behaviour. This information will not come as a surprise to most people.

Drinking tends to fuel higher risk and aggressive behaviour. Research has also shown that after drinking, people are more likely to make mistakes, are less concerned with making mistakes, and are less likely to take steps to stop themselves from making mistakes.[2] Other studies have shown that alcohol impairs performance in nearly every domain. For example, in a report of business negotiators, after alcohol consumption, negotiators were more aggressive, made more mistakes, and reached poorer outcomes than the sober negotiators in the study. Interestingly, the intoxicated negotiators were also unaware that alcohol had affected their performance.[3]

Fine. Alcohol impairs performance and judgement. It gets darker during the nighttime, British people like to complain about the weather, and crocodiles are not good house pets. We know this, without being told again. However, the combination of alcohol, social media and the workplace still causes trouble for many people.

Organizations cannot always keep people from making bad decisions, and adults are responsible for their own decisions and behaviour. That means that organizations should have clear guidelines about what types of behaviour are desirable and acceptable (we outline this more specifically later in this chapter).

Alcohol-related posts can damage job prospects

In other chapters we discuss how employers or recruiters view certain social media activity (Chapters 22 and 23). Whether or not employers are allowed to evaluate prospective employees based on their social media activity, some certainly will and do. Some of the most common red flags that recruiters identify when screening prospective employees are alcohol and drug use, political rants and extreme views.

One of the most common causes for concern was seeing many photos of a prospective employee with alcohol, too much alcohol, or clearly intoxicated. This is easier to identify in photos, but alcohol use can often be apparent in text-based posts too. Whether or not they are a sign of intoxication, recruiters tend to see long rambling posts, belligerent content or incoherent activity in the small hours of the morning as a significant warning.

Of course, it may be unfair (and potentially illegal) to evaluate employees based on their behavior outside of the workplace, and some people might not want their employer reading the point they were trying to make on Twitter at 2 am Wednesday morning. Legally, the employer could be in a bit of hot water if they make an employment decision based on that activity that is irrelevant to job performance. Practically speaking, though, posting that information publicly online is extremely unwise.

Don't bring your whole self to work

How does someone keep their personal life and their work life separate in the age of social media? Where is the boundary between personal social interaction online and business communications? There certainly has to be some sort of boundary because clients, colleagues and customers will certainly search online for people they know professionally.

There is much discussion about work–life balance and bringing your whole self to work in the age of social media. The idea promotes a rather rosy view of the world where people's personal and work lives intersect nicely, business and personal relationships overlap, and everyone can be happy without hiding behind a professional veneer.

However, 'bringing your whole self to work' is an over-optimistic approach and one of those naive workplace platitudes. The workplace shouldn't really be a place to bring out all of your insecurities, emotional instabilities and psychodramas. What if a person's 'whole self' includes being a morally questionable drunken lout? They may be great fun on the weekend, but that shouldn't be brought into the workplace. Bringing your whole self to work might seem like a nice idea, but it could also be a quick way to get fired.

There is a very large and very ambiguous grey area with social media. A person's social media activity, when public, does have the potential to impact their relationships at work, and their overall work. This can be especially concerning when people write social media posts about their workplace, their colleagues, clients or boss. Writing in the *New York Times*, Rafael

Gomez, an employment and labour lawyer, writes, 'Social media simply cannot grant employees immunity from careless posting.'[4]

It is safe to assume that anything posted publicly on social media will eventually be noticed by someone. When many of the person's contacts or friends on a social media profile are from the same company or office, it is also fairly safe to assume that all the related content can or will be discussed in the office – especially when colleagues are tagged in the posts or photos. This is where alcohol in the mix can make everything a bit more caustic.

Employers will also be keenly aware that the behaviour of their employees reflects on the company overall, as well as a line manager's decision-making capabilities. That's why it is so important for a company to have clear social media guidelines.

It may also be helpful to define boundaries between personal and business communications. In the same way that the way people talk to their friends in the pub may not translate into a work environment, the way people interact with their friends on social media will not always translate very well into digital communications in a professional environment.

Don't bring the spam to work

There is an online phenomenon in which people choose to deliberately post irrelevant or low quality and tangential content in discussions, often with a bit of aggression thrown in the mix. The internet term for this kind of activity is 'shitposting'. This is the kind of behaviour that often goes hand-in-hand with alcohol and social media. It's a bit like going to the pub and having a very wide-ranging discussion without a clear train of thought. If a group of friends enjoys doing this, that's perfectly fine, but it is less likely to be greeted warmly in the workplace.

Or think of it like the friend or family member who likes to drink too much at a dinner party, who likes to derail the conversation, start arguments and generally cause a bit of chaos for the fun of it. Maybe it's a group of friends who like to be a bit silly online and have developed their own in-jokes and ways of interacting with each other. The problem comes when people don't realize they need to draw a line between how they communicate in the workplace and how they might interact with others outside it.

This is another reason why it is important for employers to have clear guidelines about professional communications. These should also clarify and explain how personal, public communications on social media can affect both the person's and the company's reputation.[5]

Recommendations for social media policy

All companies should have a social media policy that covers social media conduct in the workplace, and describes what kind of online behaviours could cause problems for the company outside it (eg photos taken while in a company uniform, personal posts to a company's page, personal posts about professional relationships).

Here are some recommendations for areas a social media policy should cover, followed by a great example from Coca-Cola's policy.

Have a clear policy for resolving disputes outside social media

Disagreements are bound to happen in the workplace, and there should be a clear and accessible way to manage these disputes in a constructive way. Complaining about colleagues, gossiping, and posting grievances on social media is much more likely to occur when employees do not have a more fair and constructive way to manage disputes and resolve problems. Effective HR and management practices can help manage this.

Clearly define what information is confidential

Certain workplace information should never be posted publicly or even privately to someone's social media page or an external site. Typically, this includes confidential information such as client information, business plans, personnel data, and intellectual property.

However, some information that seems innocuous may also be confidential – for example, accidentally revealing location history, meeting dates, diary appointments or tagging other people in a post has the potential to give away sensitive information (see Chapter 17). Clearly define what information is considered confidential to avoid employees making innocent mistakes.

Designate a specific person to answer questions

Many people find it difficult to keep track of all the information they are sharing online, some people will find social media etiquette and company policies confusing. Designate a specific person who can give friendly advice about company policy and social media. It should be someone who is both knowledgeable and approachable.

It's great to have someone to ask about these topics, and employees will appreciate being able to access the advice. It also disqualifies the old 'No one told me that was a bad idea before I did it' argument.

Provide positive examples of how to engage with others online

This is particularly important, because providing models of desirable and effective behaviour in the workplace tends to be more effective than long lists and policy manuals of no-nos. Give examples of how people have managed conflict, used social media to get information effectively, or used the technology in an admirable way.

Remember that even people who have a great deal of experience with personal social media may have never used it for professional purposes before.

Clearly explain what is illegal and unethical online

There are some obvious examples here – no hate speech, no bigoted language, and don't threaten or harass people online. But there may be more nuanced issues, such as how and where employees can use the company logo or copyrighted materials online. Can employees use a picture of themselves in a company uniform or at a company-branded site on their social media page? If so, are there added expectations for their conduct online?

Clarify the consequences of certain actions

This is no different to any other workplace policy. Stealing, bullying, or harassment in the workplace should all carry consequences, and this should apply equally if bad behaviour occurs on social media.

Minor mistakes or slip-ups may only require a quick chat, and an explanation of how to handle the situation better next time.

Embed company culture in the policy

Social media policies can vary widely depending on the job and the responsibilities involved. Professions with a duty of care such as teachers, psychologists, physicians and support workers should have stricter codes of conduct governing their behaviour both inside and outside the workplace.

For some professions it is more important to err on the side of caution, while others can take a much more relaxed approach. Some companies will encourage employees to have a more playful and flexible approach to social media, which is great – but the boundaries of acceptable behaviour should still be clear.

Coca-Cola has a good example of a social media policy, with general guidelines that reference more specific policy documents.[6] They are also regularly updated (if your company's social media policy is five years old or more, it's definitely time to revisit it).

The guidelines are as follows:

1 Our Company's Information Protection Policy, Insider Trading Policy, and other policies still apply.

2 You are responsible for your actions. We encourage you to get online and have fun but use sound judgement and common sense.

3 You are an important ambassador for our Company's brands, and you're encouraged to promote them as long as you make sure you disclose that you are affiliated with the Company. How you disclose can depend on the platform, but the disclosure should be clear and in proximity to the message itself.

4 When you see posts or commentary on topics that require subject matter expertise, such as ingredients, obesity, the Company's environmental impacts, or the Company's financial performance, avoid the temptation to respond to these directly unless you respond with approved messaging the Company has prepared for those topics. When in doubt, contact your local Public Affairs and Communications director.

5 Be conscientious when mixing your business and personal lives be sure to know your work group's policies regarding personal use of social media at work or on Company devices.

Conclusion

This chapter has a slightly more ambiguous conclusion than some others with very clear and direct recommendations. Issues around potentially harmful employee behaviour and social media are more complex when alcohol is thrown into the mix.

There are two firm recommendations for employers, and one for individuals. Firstly, employers should have a clear policy in place that outlines what behaviour is acceptable on social media, both within the workplace and outside it. Employees should have a clear picture of what kind of public online behaviour could have a negative effect on their work or their employer.

Secondly, employers should be very cautious about encouraging or facilitating excessive alcohol consumption in conjunction with any work activities. Having a Christmas party where you expect people to overindulge? Fine – take the normal and reasonable precautious that are necessary when serving alcohol, and suspend work activities for the duration, including social media, work emails, and conversations with clients.

For employees in the workplace, the simple message is: Don't be a drunken idiot and then post it online, and don't mix intoxication with your work. Adults can make their own decisions and deal with the consequences of their own actions, and we don't want to recommend heavy-handed employer regulations or policing employee behaviour outside of the workplace. That tends to be counterproductive and makes the workplace less enjoyable for people who can responsibility manage their alcohol intake and behaviour on social media.

One final message should be clear. The cocktail of one-part work, one-part alcohol, and a dash of social media can be a risky and inadvisable concoction.

Notes

1   Gan, G et al (2014) Alcohol-induced impairment of inhibitory control is linked to attenuated brain responses in right fronto-temporal cortex, *Biological Psychiatry*, 76 (**9**), pp 698–707

2   Bartholow, B D et al (2012) Alcohol effects on performance monitoring and adjustment: Affect modulation and impairment of evaluative cognitive control, *Journal of Abnormal Psychology*, 121 (**1**), pp 173–86

3   Schweitzer, M E and Gomberg, L E (2001) The impact of alcohol on negotiator behaviour: experimental evidence, *Journal of Applied Social Psychology*, 31 (**10**), pp 2095–126

4   Employees must practice caution when using social media: www.nytimes.com/roomfordebate/2013/04/02/should-social-media-activity-cost-you-your-job/employees-must-practice-caution-when-using-social-media (archived at https://perma.cc/T7RX-A6SF)

5   Hendriks, H et al (2018) Social drinking on social media: Content analysis of the social aspects of alcohol-related posts on Facebook and Instagram, *Journal of Medical Internet Research*, 20 (6), p 226

6   Social media principles: www.coca-colacompany.com/stories/online-social-media-principles (archived at https://perma.cc/W7K7-C3Z4)

DIGITAL NATIVES ARE ALL SOCIAL MEDIA EXPERTS

*Although there may be some crossover in knowledge
and experience, don't assume experience in using social media
for personal communication will translate into expertise in its
professional use.*

Introduction

There is a general assumption that groups of people of a similar age share certain traits, values and skills. One common belief is that because younger people grew up with computers, smartphones, easy access to the internet and social media, they are naturally proficient at using all of the above – and the insinuation is often that this relationship between young people and technology is toxic. For example, you may see headlines such as 'Social media is as harmful as alcohol and drugs for Millennials'.[1]

A similar assumption is that all young people are experts in the domains of technology and social media. While coverage of the effects of social media is often negative, a corresponding assumption is often made that the under-30s are generally more social media-savvy[2] and use this technology as though it's second nature. Media discussion takes on the topic with headlines such as 'Millennials and Generation Z interact more through phones and apps than in real life',[3] and 'Smartphones are destroying my generation'.[4]

There are two major problems with this assumption:

1 This stereotype, like all stereotypes, is not universally true for all members of a group.

2 Personal use of social media does not necessarily translate into effective use of social media for business.

We will discuss these two points in more detail throughout this chapter. But first, it's necessary to remember that someone's age is not a very good predictor of their proficiency in any particular skill.

The problem with age stereotypes

Most stereotypes based on age or generational differences are false. There certainly are many young people who are proficient social media users, and of course there are older people who have little to no understanding of social media. However, assuming that age always predicts social media proficiency in the workplace is a mistake.

Most of the stereotypes about younger (and older) workers do not stand up to scrutiny. The book *Myths of Work* takes a systemic approach to debunking common myths about younger (and older) generations.[5] Younger workers are sometimes assumed to be lazy, social media-obsessed narcissists, while older workers are painted as dogmatic, resistant to change and slow to learn. The research from hundreds of scientific studies looking at hundreds of thousands of workers finds no evidence that either stereotype is true. The book concludes: 'There are no significant generational differences in the workplace and there are far better factors to measure people on, such as personality, intelligence, individual motivation, skills and experience.'

The problem for business is that making decisions based on flawed assumptions leads to mistakes. When hiring employees who are responsible for a business's social media, it is always far more effective to hire the most skilled person instead of basing your hiring decision on age.

Personal use vs business aptitude

Let's say someone is a great cook. They cook every day, love doing it and are extremely proficient in the kitchen. Could this skill easily translate into a successful business? Maybe. But there is a significant gap between the skills and knowledge it takes to be a great cook, and the skills and knowledge required to run a successful restaurant. Can the person prep and cook in volume? Can they adapt the food for people with allergies and different dietary requirements? Can they manage inventory and costs? What about hiring, managing and developing staff? Do they have the skills required for sales and customer service? Perhaps they can translate their personal aptitude into business success, but this shouldn't be assumed.

The same is true when translating any aptitude into business success. Social media is not an exception. Any sort of technology can be used in many different ways. Someone may be very comfortable working with computers and information technology, but be completely clueless when it comes to managing an Excel spreadsheet.

Others may use social media daily or even hourly for personal use. They may use a number of different platforms to communicate with friends and family, consume digital media and buy products online. This familiarity with social media may be an advantage that can translate into using social media for business purposes, but there is no guarantee.

In some cases, people who are regular social media users and consumers may have actually picked up habits that are acceptable for personal social media use, but unacceptable for business purposes.

Separating the personal and workplace spheres

There's another interesting trend that suggests the increase in social media related to work may actually discourage the use of some social media. Recent research amongst younger people also shows there may be a coming backlash in younger user's perception of social media.

Research conducted by the Headmasters' and Headmistresses' Conference (HMC) and Digital Awareness UK found significant distrust of social media for personal use. Nearly two-thirds (63 per cent) of students said they would not care if social media did not exist 71 per cent reported taking long breaks or 'digital detoxes', and more than half reported experiencing abuse online.[6]

There may be more going on here. Now, many people are required to use social media for some or all of their work. Some reports have suggested that using social media for work can discourage people from using social media for personal use – for example, one respondent to the HMC survey said:

'Because social media is my job I have to cut back, so I don't look at my Instagram after hours and I don't use Facebook unless I need to contact someone, or for work. I find this allows me to create clarity between my online and offline worlds. It's draining to be constantly connected, because sometimes I just want silence.'[7]

There is an interesting psychological concept at play here called the 'over-justification effect', which was initially described in 1971 by Edward Deci.[8] In the original experiments, participants were given games to play during the study, and were also allowed (but not required) to play the games while taking a break. Some participants were paid to play the game while others were not. Participants who were paid to play the game were far less likely to continue playing the game during their break than participants who were not paid until after the study was over.

The results demonstrate how paying people to complete an activity actually makes them less motivated to participate once the rewards are taken away. This is because there are two main types of motivation, which are quite distinctive:

- **Intrinsic motivators** motivate people to do work for some sort of internal reward. This can include things like a feeling of achievement at completing work that is challenging, recognition, being given responsibility, or the opportunity to do something meaningful. They bring satisfaction arising from the intrinsic conditions of the job itself.

- **Extrinsic motivators** are factors such as job security, salary, fringe benefits, work conditions, good pay, paid insurance and holidays, and so on. These tend not to give a strong sense of satisfaction, though dissatisfaction often results from their absence. These are outside of the value of the work itself, but are a key reward in most jobs.

Research has shown the over-justification effect arises consistently for all types of people, with different types of rewards and in different situations.[9,10] Essentially, paying people to do something makes them less likely to participate in that activity in the future if it does not come with a financial reward.

This is an important concept when discussing the overlap between social media manager's work and their personal lives. Although there may be some crossover in knowledge and experience, don't assume experience in using social media for personal communication will translate into expertise in its professional use. The two different domains may work happily in concert, but they do not always.

Social media policies and onboarding

Most workplaces have policies on a variety of issues that need to be monitored and regulated. Companies have policies about recruitment and retention, use of business resources, bullying and sexual harassment, data protection, interactions with customers and a host of other domains. The same should be true about social media policy (see Chapter 18 for a sample social media policy), and these policies should be integrated with others.

Recruitment and onboarding is a good place to start. Employee orientation processes should provide an introduction to social media policies covering introductory topics. If employees are allowed to use social media during work hours, it should cover what sort of use is appropriate. For example, recruiters will likely spend a great deal of time on social media at work, but should probably not be posting political memes on the company accounts.

Development and training initiatives should assess social media competency, and work to build employee social media skills and understanding in a business context. For example, the style and content of work-related social media activity should be consistent with the company's objectives and values. This needs to be defined, because social media activity will vary with company culture. Some companies may prefer more informal and light-hearted use of social media, while others will want to ensure employees are more professional and restrained.

Privacy and data protection policy must take social media use into account. Many companies have found, to their detriment, that the barrier between internal company information and its employees' social media use is rather too porous. Companies must ensure all employees understand what can and cannot be shared publicly on social media.

Never assume that any employee, irrespective of their age, knows everything about social media. Even for those recruits who have a great deal of experience with it in a personal capacity, you cannot assume they understand all the etiquette and policy for social media use in a business context.

Conclusion

Social media is now part of many people's personal and social lives, and it is closely interconnected with many business functions. But just because many younger people use social media, do not assume all young people are proficient. Avoid making assumptions about any employee or prospective employee's proficiency based on their age alone.

Assess and develop the social media literacy of prospective employees and of workers within the company, just as with any other workplace competency.

Notes

1 Social media is as harmful as alcohol and drugs for millennials: https://theconversation.com/social-media-is-as-harmful-as-alcohol-and-drugs-for-millennials-78418 (archived at https://perma.cc/9X2N-ZA7C)

2 MacRae, I and Furnham, A (2017a) *Motivation and Performance: A guide to motivating a diverse workforce*, Kogan Page, London

3 Millennials and Generation Z interact more through phones and apps than in real life, report finds: www.independent.co.uk/life-style/gadgets-and-tech/news/millennials-generation-z-smartphone-habits-apps-communications-real-life-a8008641.html (archived at https://perma.cc/RF7G-XXNY)

4 Smartphones are destroying my generation: www.nationalreview.com/2017/08/millennial-smartphone-usage-social-media-loneliness/ (archived at https://perma.cc/XL6L-4FXV)

5 MacRae, I and Furnham, A (2017b) *Myths of Work: The stereotypes and assumptions holding your organization back*, Kogan Page, London

6 Parent/pupil digital behaviour poll – Media briefing: www.hmc.org.uk/blog/parentpupil-digital-behaviour-poll-media-briefing/ (archived at https://perma.cc/JNW7-FWCB)

7 Why we Millennials are so happy to be free of social media tyranny: www.theguardian.com/media/2017/nov/12/millennials-backlash-social-media-facebook-instagram-snapchat (archived at https://perma.cc/6HTL-E7AJ)

8 Deci, E L (1972) Effects of externally mediated rewards on intrinsic motivation, *Journal of Personality and Social Psychology,* 18, pp 105–115

9 Tang, S and Hall, V C (1995) The over justification effect: A meta-analysis, *Applied Cognitive Psychology*, 9 (5), pp 365–404

10 Cerasoli, C P, Nicklin, J M and Ford, M T (2014) Intrinsic motivation and extrinsic incentives jointly predict performance: A 40-year meta-analysis, *Psychological Bulletin*, 140, pp 980–1008

SOCIAL MEDIA INFLUENCERS ARE A NEW PHENOMENON

*There is nothing particularly new about celebrities
setting or defining trends and then selling the associated
products or services. Prominent and popular people who
can reach an audience have always been paid to promote
products or services.*

Introduction

Whether or not someone is an 'influencer' typically seems to be defined by the number of followers they have on social media. A 2017 article in British *Vogue* discusses how someone's follower count is seen as their 'currency'.[1] Apparently, the number of followers is far more important to an influencer's status than past work, successes or other common metrics that would be included in a traditional CV.

It's easy to be dismissive of influencers by looking at some of the less successful examples, and like any business there are far more stories of failure to launch than success. However, according to the *New York Times*, successful influencers 'are essentially one-person start-ups, and the best ones can spot trends, experiment relentlessly with new formats and platforms'. They are a personal brand, their identity, attitudes and their bodies highly sought-after marketing platforms. They 'pay close attention to their channel analytics and figure out how to distinguish themselves in a crowded media environment – all while churning out a constant stream of new content'.[2]

Influencing people has always been more of an art than a science, so it is not especially easy to come up with a clear metrics that define an 'influencer'. Someone could have millions of followers, but exert very little sway on their following (and may not even want to!). whereas a small circle of dedicated persuaders can exert a great deal of influence.

It can be useful to look at the different kinds of influence from people who create, develop, disseminate and endorse messages. In his 2000 book *The Tipping Point*, Malcom Gladwell talks about a relatively small group of socially-savvy and skilled people who tend to have a significant influence.[3] Gladwell sorts these people into three different categories:

- **Connectors** have wide communication networks and can influence a large number of people. Gladwell explains these people in terms of traditional networks and direct interpersonal connections. However, it is easy to see how this idea is applicable to social media, where people can broadcast information to hundreds, thousands or even millions online.

- **Mavens** are the specialists and experts who are the first to learn about new information, trends or ideas. They are knowledgeable, tend to be early adopters, and actively share their expertise or experience with others.

- **Salespeople** are persuasive and charismatic and are good at convincing other people in their network. In 2000, Gladwell focused on the importance of non-verbal cues in convincing and persuading, but it is easy to see how this would be equally important on social media. Indeed, platforms like Instagram are designed to send messages using non-verbal cues and messages about someone's lifestyle, ideas and aspirations.

> **Influencer**: a person with the ability to have an effect on others and convince others to buy a specific product, adopt a certain idea or behave in a certain way by promotion or recommendation on social media.

Ambiguous definitions

Given the ambiguity in how the term is used, there has been a search for clarity in defining exactly what makes someone an 'influencer'. In the summer of 2019, there seemed to finally be an answer on the matter. 'Anyone with more than 30,000 followers considered a celebrity, advertising watchdog rules,' read the headline in the *Telegraph* and the *Daily Mail* reported the same.[4,5]

This could be a useful rule of thumb – but did the UK's Advertising Standards Authority (ASA) really come up with a number to define what constituted a celebrity or an influencer on social media? No. But why let the details get in the way of a good headline?

In this case, someone with about 30,000 followers promoted sleeping pills on their Instagram page. After complaints, the ASA was asked to conclude whether it breached their rules on celebrity endorsements of health and medical products. The company that manufactures the sleeping pills argued that the influencer's following was too small to have an impact on consumer behaviour (which seems like a strange defence – why advertise with an influencer you don't think has any influence?).

The ASA was not stating a definitive number of followers. They were just considering whether, in this single case, the influencer and the company were breaching the regulations on endorsing medical products. As it turns out, they were. Haley Bosher at Brunel University writes, 'The ASA did not dream up a magic number of followers that somehow defines a celebrity – it simply determined that in this case, around 30,000 followers were enough to constitute a celebrity endorsement of the product.'[6]

In this case, the message was that even for a person with a relatively small number of followers (in this case, 30,000), advertising rules on celebrity endorsement will apply.

The rise of the social influencer

Traditional marketing platforms and techniques are still big business. It's still a $100 billion industry in the US, and although the spending is slowly contracting every year, it is not going to disappear. Print marketing is falling quickly, while TV and radio marketing seems to be waning gradually – see Figure 20.1.

2019 is predicted to be the year that digital ad spending surpasses advertising spending on traditional media, as shown in Figure 20.2. More than half of this digital advertising spending goes through two companies: Google and Facebook.

The shift in advertising spend means that there is more money to be made in social media advertising, and the new generation of online influencers are taking note. They are building businesses that take advantage of, and continue to fuel, the trend.

Figure 20.1   Changes in spending on traditional marketing mediums in the US

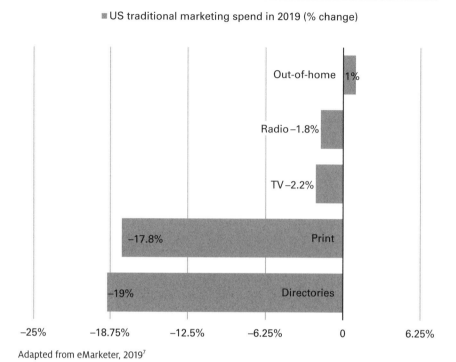

Adapted from eMarketer, 2019[7]

Figure 20.2   Projections for traditional vs digital ad spending in the US, 2018–21

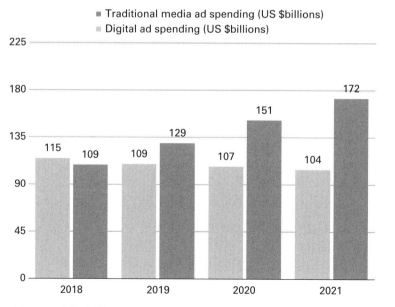

Adapted from eMarketer, 2019

As traditional media loses viewers to online platforms, the advertising money will continue shifting towards where the potential customers are. As we've explained in other chapters, social media provides huge advertising platforms that can deftly target very specific groups and audiences. On social networks, people already organize themselves into groups with similar values, ideologies, styles and consumer behaviours (see Chapter 28).

The influencer is another way to reach these groups. Successful influencers have turned a particular, contrived version of their life into a 'brand'. Influencers then, are the perfect mouthpiece for brands to sell their products.

It would be extremely unwise to write off influencers on social media. Although there is a great deal of superficiality and silly antics, a lot of influencers are hard at work, and influencers on social media are a dominant force in shaping culture, trends and consumer behaviour. There have always been 'influencers'. Movie stars, television personalities, radio hosts and political pundits have always shaped culture and trends, often backed by big money. We just haven't always called them influencers. The new generation of Instagram, YouTube and TikTok stars are, in many ways, very similar.

When it is done in a well-organized and concerted way, social media influencers can generate a huge amount of buzz around a product or topic that seems organic. Social media platforms, for many people, are a fairly casual and informal communication network. Trends that emerge can seem to appear from nowhere. When the top influencers all jump in on a topic it can generate that feeling of 'Everyone is talking about this'. In reality, it is more likely to be because one company is paying a lot of different influential people to be talking about it.

TikTok is a new video sharing social media application that took off in 2019. It could be that it's just such an interesting platform that it naturally became popular, or it could be that top influencers and social media platforms have been bombarding viewers with adverts.

What does it take to make a new social media platform take off? Do these viral sensations appear out of a good idea and a shoestring budget? Of course not. According to the *Wall Street Journal*, we can put TikTok's swift rise in 2019 down to a £776 million marketing budget from Chinese parent company Bytedance.[8]

Most interestingly, we can see how this budget relies on the already-available infrastructure of social media marketing giants. The tailored advertising and massive networks of influencers and content creators provides the environment for a company's product to go viral, or for an unknown business to become a household name, in a relatively short space of time, if the marketing department is prepared to pay for it.

As the *Wall Street Journal* reports, TikTok became the first major Chinese consumer technology company to break into the US market. In turn, TikTok will become another massive digital advertising platform, targeting the lucrative youth market. The case of TikTok shows how social media continues to fuel digital advertising industry growth. And as the developed markets become saturated, the social media companies turn their attention towards developing markets.

We must be cautious, however, about industry predictions that forecast continued exponential growth. As economic cycles tend to remind us every decade, rapid expansion and unchecked spending eventually comes to an end. As the social media companies expand, rise, and fall, they can switch from growing into new markets into corporate cannibalism. Some of them are bound to go the way of Sun Microsystems, Compaq and Vine.

All publicity is good publicity

Although all clever marketers want to go viral with a great message, advert or campaign, it doesn't usually happen organically. It takes a great deal of planning and money to make something a viral hit. Spontaneity takes a lot of effort online.

In rare and fortunate occasions, products can go viral without a huge investment of time and money. This is the exception rather than the rule, but it certainly is possible. Attracting the attention of an undisciplined or impulsive high-profile influencer can also result in a lot of free publicity!

That's why a competitive sport, of sorts, has arisen that we'll call Trump-baiting. One quick way to get international media attention is to feature in one of the American President's erratic Twitter episodes. This influential septuagenarian loves a social media clapback, and because he is such a divisive figure, being either praised or insulted by Donald Trump can be a marketing boon.

Authors critical of Donald Trump have found that by participating in creative Trump-baiting, they can inspire an angry response from the President that can help a book shoot up the New York Times bestseller list. They just dangle a few choice insults about the President's intelligence or temperament in front of him like a lukewarm cheeseburger and wait for a nibble.

Various authors have got attention, from Michael Wolff ('a total loser who made up stories to sell this really boring and untruthful book')[9] to Bob Woodward (whose 'book is a total scam. I don't talk the way I'm quoted. If I did, I would not have been elected President')[10] and James Comey, who features regularly: 'Shadey James Comey can Leak and Lie and make lots of money from a third-rate book (that should never have been written).'[11] For a President with such high unfavourability ratings, many people will latch on to anything that he dislikes.

While this may not be constructive criticism, it certainly is free publicity. Any person or company with a large social media following or a position of influence would be wise to learn from this. Sometimes ranting *against* someone or something on social media, clapping back, or heating up the debate online actually serves to promote it more. It may seem to be a natural response to want to defend yourself, your brand or your company online. And while social media can be a great way of responding to constructive customer complaints, be wary of amplifying negative publicity.

Conclusion

Influencers are a growing force in advertising and the digital economy. Personal brands connected with specific styles, beliefs, ideologies and lifestyles are a natural partner for targeted advertising. If social media creates filter bubbles, influencers are the quickest way to get to the centre of any bubble.

There is nothing particularly new about celebrities setting or defining trends and then selling the associated products or services. They may be on different platforms like YouTube and Instagram instead of on the radio and television, but the effect is largely the same. Prominent and popular people who can reach an audience have always been paid to promote products or services.

The advice in other chapters holds it is possible to build up a following over time organically. This takes a great deal of time, dedication, hard work and carving out a niche. It is also possible to break into a market as a viral sensation if you have billions to spend on online advertising. Some of the players may be new, but the game has not changed much.

Notes

1   What is an influencer? www.vogue.co.uk/article/what-is-an-influencer (archived at https://perma.cc/L8AS-G93H)

2   Don't scoff at influencers. They're taking over the world: www.nytimes.com/2019/07/16/technology/vidcon-social-media-influencers.html (archived at https://perma.cc/3K9Q-UWU9)

3 Gladwell, M (2000) *The Tipping Point: How little things can make a big difference*, Little, Brown, Boston, MA

4 Anyone with more than 30,000 social media followers considered a celebrity, advertising watchdog rules: www.telegraph.co.uk/news/2019/07/02/anyone-30000-social-media-followers-considered-celebrity-advertising (archived at https://perma.cc/J4QS-3HJF)

5 Anyone with at least 30,000 followers on social media is officially a 'celebrity', UK advertising regulator reveals: www.dailymail.co.uk/sciencetech/article-7212745/Anyone-30-000-followers-social-media-officially-celebrity.html (archived at https://perma.cc/PLM6-8PFF)

6 Instagram influencers: No, having 30,000 followers does not make you a celebrity: www.brunel.ac.uk/news-and-events/news/articles/Instagram-influencers-no-having-30000-followers-does-not-make-you-a-celebrity (archived at https://perma.cc/QFS7-9X3Y)

7 US digital ad spending will surpass traditional in 2019: www.emarketer.com/content/us-digital-ad-spending-will-surpass-traditional-in-2019 (archived at https://perma.cc/5PG6-UDY3)

8 TikTok's videos are goofy. Its strategy to dominate social media is serious: www.wsj.com/articles/tiktoks-videos-are-goofy-its-strategy-to-dominate-social-media-is-serious-11561780861 (archived at https://perma.cc/ZFL7-73GN)

9 Retrieved from https://twitter.com/realdonaldtrump/status/949498795074736129 (archived at https://perma.cc/CC3Z-9SUW)

10 Retrieved from https://twitter.com/realdonaldtrump/status/1039124232368730114 (archived at https://perma.cc/8QN7-SVFG)

11 Retrieved from https://twitter.com/realdonaldtrump/status/987278269765517312 (archived at https://perma.cc/BQ7S-KY6Q)

MYTH
21

PEOPLE HAVE DIFFERENT PERSONALITIES ON SOCIAL MEDIA

The way people think and behave on social media
is influenced by their underlying, stable, personality traits,
and not the other way around.

Introduction

Social media websites have different cultures, norms and types of behaviour that are encouraged or discouraged (see Chapter 28). So if people act a bit differently depending which site they are on, social media must be changing people's personalities online, right? A 2011 article in *Forbes* entitled 'Multiple personalities and social media: The many faces of me' makes that claim.[1] It suggests that people segment their personalities, and slot them into different online locations.

Others would argue that social media profiles are more like an airbrushed caricature of people. This is certainly true when a profile has a certain format that highlights specific information, and omits a great deal. The criticism is that people tend to highlight and share the more exciting elements of their lives, while glossing over some less attractive features.

While it may be true that people tend to accentuate the positive, and omit some of the more mundane, uninteresting or unattractive parts of their lives and personalities on social media this is no different to what people do in their everyday offline lives. Psychologists call it 'impression management', and it's a conscious or subconscious effort to present ourselves to other people in a certain light.

Social media may colour how people represent themselves, and highlight certain aspects of their personality and behaviour, but it doesn't change it. Some people have a jaundiced view of how people portray themselves on social media, while other may have rose-tinted spectacles. Yet all behaviour on social media actually gives us useful and measurable insight into a person's personality. Instead of obscuring or changing people's personality, social media actually allows us a better window into understanding how personality manifests in different environments.

Can you measure personality?

Personality is used to describe many different things, and on social media the term is used quite loosely. For example, 'personality quizzes' use a few lighthearted questions to provide a vague description of people – often matching them to characters from a movie or television series. In this broad sense, personality is used to refer to anything from character traits to motivation, values or ways of interacting with other people.

When we talk about personality in this chapter, we should make clear we are talking about a psychological definition of the term. Personality is 'a stable pattern of thinking, feeling and acting'.[2] The word 'stable' is particularly important in this definition, because it means that an individual's personality remains more or less unchanged throughout their adult life.

When we measure personality, we can get insights into how people operate, and even predict how successful they are likely to be at work.[3] Indeed, personality is one of the best predictors of workplace performance. Their personality and behaviour online tends to be a fairly good indicator of how they will act outside of cyberspace as well.

There are six personality traits we can use to look at behaviours, and these behaviours are actually quite consistent online and offline.[4]

Personality traits remain stable over an adult's lifespan and in different areas of people's lives, whether they are online or offline, on social media or in a physical office.[6,7] People may behave a bit differently in different situations – for example, they might act differently with their boss while at work than with their colleagues in the pub after work, or talk in a different way in a Twitter DM than with their grandmother. But these are minor changes, not radical shifts in personality.

Table 21.1   The six personality traits

	FACTOR DEFINERS			
	Low		**High**	
	Perceived Positives	Perceived Negatives	Perceived Positives	Perceived Negatives
Conscientiousness	Easy-going Lenient Flexible Spontaneous Relaxed Considerate	Careless Unmotivated Impulsive Lax Idle Disorganised	Disciplined Self-motivated Organized Determined Logical Persistent	Obsessive Perfectionistic Rigid Inflexible Indecisive Critical
Adjustment	Sensitive Responsive Perceptive Passionate Emotive Expressive	Emotional Imational Neurotic Self-conscious Moody Compulsive	Controlled Peaceful Even-tempered Self-confident Composed Emotionally stable	Indifferent Unresponsive Distant Serious Aloof Cold
Curiosity	Focused Traditional Dependable Sensible Reliable Indifferent	Closed-minded Conventional Disinterested Suspicious Unadventurous Obstinate	Innovative Creative Open-minded Attentive Interested Inquisitive	Unpredictable Inconsistent Eccentric Easily-distracted Unfocused Intrusive
Risk Approach	Cautious Careful Vigilant Supportive Obliging Harmonious	Avoidant Risk-averse Hesitant Reactive Passive Apprehensive	Bold Tactical Proactive Candid Courageous Self-assured	Confrontational Imposing Reckless Blunt Insensitive Arrogant

(continued)

Table 21.1 (Continued)

FACTOR DEFINERS				
	Low		High	
	Perceived Positives	Perceived Negatives	Perceived Positives	Perceived Negatives
Ambiguity Acceptance	Deliberate	Predictable	Tolerant	Unclear
	Orderly	Stubborn	Versatile	Erratic
	Consistent	Fussy	Analytical	Illogical
	Methodical	Inflexible	Resourceful	Abstract
	Straightforward	Blinkered	Adaptable	Vague
	Precise	Simplistic	Considered	Confusing
Competitiveness	Cooperative	Unenthusiastic	Goal-oriented	Ruthless
	Amenable	Timid	Ambitious	Aggressive
	Accommodating	Satisfied		Antagonistic
	Modest	Submissive	Striving	Unyielding
	Undemanding	Quiet	Driven	Harsh
	Easy-going	Apathetic	Assertive	Hostile
			Eager	

People adapt to their situations and the people around them, but how they behave in these situations are guided by their underlying personality traits. If that is true in real-world situations, it holds true in cyberspace.

Behaviour on social media

People's personalities are generally quite stable over time. Personality impacts how people assess and understand different situations and environments, which is why people tend to behave very similarly and in a fairly predictable way when they are working on similar tasks. Put a person in unfamiliar circumstances, such as a new job, and they may behave differently. Yet personality gives a good indication on how they will react to things like stress, novelty, ambiguity, risk and competition in a new environment.

Researchers have found that people's behaviour on social media closely aligns with their personality traits.[8,9] The same traits that are influencing their behaviour in the real world are influencing their behaviour in these digital spaces.[10,11] The nature of social media actually makes this relatively easy to test, because many people post a huge amount of personal information, photos, and social interaction online.

This is one myth that is relatively easy to dispel, because there is a substantial amount of research with clear conclusions. Personality traits are stable and measurable, and are directly linked to behaviour both online and offline.

Assessing personality

Understanding personality and its connection with behaviour both online and offline offers significant potential benefits for understanding people at work. Personality acts as a long-term guide to employee performance and potential, and therefore can be useful for identifying, developing and retaining high-potential employees.[12]

Finding those with potential

There are talented people out there, but is not always easy to spot them. When businesses are looking for prospective employees, they want to find the people who are likely to perform most effectively in the job. Skills, knowledge and work history can typically serve as an indicator of past performance, but assessing personality provides a better guide to a prospective employee's future potential.

The way people behave in the office, and the way they use digital technology and communicate with colleagues using internal or external social media, offers a good insight into their workplace potential. See more about internal social media networks in Chapter 13.

Developing those with potential

Personality is an excellent indicator of potential development trajectories. Promotions into new positions often involve learning a host of new skills, developing new relationships and mastering the role.

When the job involves a fundamentally different set of competencies (for example, moving from a specialist or technical role into a managerial role), personality is actually a better indicator of potential success in the new role than previous performance in a very different role.

Retaining those with potential

It is rather common for organizations to neglect the fact that commitment to a job and to an organization is not automatic. Keeping existing employees should be as much as a priority as finding and developing talented new staff. In many cases, it is actually more important.

Long-term employees already represent a huge investment, and losing them represents a significant cost. Understanding employee personality and how that fits with their work is essential for keeping staff motivated and productive at work. Employee retention takes ongoing effort, but is certainly worth the investment of time and resources. Social media and digital communication networks are an important part of this (see also Chapters 6, 13 and 23).

Assessing personality offers a unique and nuanced opportunity to predict both performance and potential at work. Measuring personality traits as stable characteristics distinguishes what cannot be taught or changed (personality) from that which can be taught, such as knowledge and experience.

Conclusion

While some of the chapters in the book may look at complex and emerging issues with slightly equivocal conclusions, the message of this chapter should be resoundingly clear. Personality does not change from day-to-day, month-to-month, or in different situations. The way people think and behave on social media is influenced by their underlying, stable, personality traits, and not the other way around.

Notes

1 Multiple personalities and social media: The many faces of me: www.forbes.com/sites/meghancasserly/2011/01/26/multiple-personalities-and-social-media-the-many-faces-of-me (archived at https://perma.cc/9TVT-H9YB)

2 MacRae, I and Furnham, A (2018) *High Potential: How to spot, manage and develop talented people at work*, Bloomsbury, London

3 Teodorescu, A, Furnham, A and MacRae, I (2017) Trait correlates of success at work, *Journal of Selection and Assessment*, 25 (1), pp 36–42

4 The secrets of the 'high potential' personality: www.bbc.com/worklife/article/20180508-the-secrets-of-the-high-potential-personality (archived at https://perma.cc/8ZVP-9M2S)

5   Thomas International Ltd: www.thomas.co (archived at https://perma.cc/P74E-BXTH)

6   Caspi, A, Roberts, B W & Shiner, R L (2005) Personality development: Stability and change, *Annual Review of Psychology*, 56, pp 453–84

7   Damian, R I *et al* (2018) Sixteen going on sixty-six: A longitudinal study of personality stability and change over 50 years, *Journal of Personality and Social Psychology* 117 (3), pp 674–95

8   Karl, K, Peluchette, J and Schaegel, C (2010) Who's posting Facebook faux pas? A cross-cultural examination of personality differences, *International Journal of Selection and Assessment*, 18, pp 174–86

9   Kluemper, d H, Rosen, P A and Mossholder, K W (2012) Social networking websites, personality ratings, and the organizational context: More than meets the eye? *Journal of Applied Psychology*, 42 (5), pp 1143–72

10   Predicting active users' personalities based on micro-blogging behaviors: https://journals.plos.org/plosone/article?id=10.1371/journal.pone.0084997 (archived at https://perma.cc/4LLL-W9N7)

11   Azucar, D, Marengo, D and Settanni, M (2018) Predicting the Big 5 personality traits from digital footprints on social media: A meta-analysis, *Personality and Individual Differences*, 124, pp 150–59

12   The four qualities it takes to become a high flyer: www.psychologytoday.com/gb/blog/fulfillment-any-age/201705/the-four-qualities-it-takes-become-high-flyer (archived at https://perma.cc/FW44-54CH)

PERSONAL INFORMATION ON SOCIAL MEDIA SHOULD NOT BE USED BY BUSINESSES

Companies that abuse their access to personal data will make people more cautious about sharing it in the future. This has the potential to make it more challenging for everyone, even those businesses that operate ethically and legally.

Introduction

There is a wealth of information available online about both people and businesses. While a small minority of people don't engage with social media, more than 75 per cent of people and 94 per cent of 18- to 24-year-olds have social media profiles.[1] Many of those people share a substantial amount of information about themselves.

Anyone who uses the internet is constantly sharing information. Chatting, emailing, researching, shopping, ordering taxis and takeaways, reading the news and posting photos so much of a person's everyday life is recorded and stored. In Chapter 24, we detail exactly how much information is held about just one person (in this case, one of the authors). But social media companies dwarf most other online organizations by the sheer volume of personal data they collect. Much of it is securely recorded and stored, but much is revealed publicly.

That means that any person or organization can access information that people post publicly on social media – platforms like Twitter, Facebook, Instagram and the others are a treasure trove of trends, public opinion, and potential customer data.

How can companies access this data, and how should organizations be using it? The debate over security and privacy is ongoing, with public opinion, public policy and corporate approaches constantly shifting. Because technology develops at a much more rapid pace than public policy or legislation, there are some large grey areas concerning how much information companies should collect (and do collect) about people.

For the sake of simplicity and clarity, we're going to discuss some of the more straightforward and ethically acceptable uses of people's information on social media.

Data collection for employee selection

Are public social media profiles fair game for recruiters and hiring managers? Can employers search social media pages and the web for information about potential job candidates? Legally, this is a grey area that varies between countries. In regions that fall under the European Union's General Data Protection Regulation (GDPR) legislation (see Chapters 8, 23 and 24), there are restrictions on what information employers can access and for what purpose. However, the rules are far more flexible outside of the European Union.

Of course using sneaky means to access this data, such as adding the person as a 'friend' without telling them why you want to access the information on their profile, is more dubious, potentially illegal under EU GDPR if a business is using deception to obtain someone's personal data, and certainly unethical.

Some social media profiles are deliberately set up for people to broadcast their information to recruiters, hiring managers and other professional audiences. LinkedIn and job search websites are examples of this. These social media platforms are set up to share work-related information such as work history, education and past employment experience.

Screening employees on social media

Most employers check prospective job candidates online before they hire them. In 2018, a YouGov poll found that 80 per cent of employers used online social media profiles to screen potential hires.[2] Other estimates suggest anywhere from 40 per cent to 70 per cent of employers screen prospective employees' social media activity.

Although exact figures aren't available, it's clear this is now a major part of the hiring process. Larger companies are more likely to check candidate's social media profiles, and more likely to filter out candidates based on what they see on social media. According to a 2018 YouGov survey, while only 11 per cent of small companies had turned down candidates after checking up on their social media, 28 per cent of larger companies had done the same.[3]

Before discussing the pros and cons, there is one fairly large elephant in the room – legality. In the US, it is legal to view any material that job candidates have posted publicly, whereas in the European Union it is not. Any area that falls under the GDPR requires that businesses obtain informed consent prior to accessing, storing or using someone's personal data.

This means that job candidates must give the prospective employer 'informed consent' before that company can review any personal data that may be available on social media and use this in evaluating their suitability for a job – even when this information is already publicly available. Best practice should involve telling prospective job candidates exactly what you are looking for, what information you might use and how the hiring decision will be made. That includes any background checks or reviews of information you might find about them online.

Another risk of using social media in job screening is that many sites include information, attitudes and opinions that are not directly related to the job. Employment law in most countries requires that employees be evaluated only on factors that are directly related to the job (called a bona fide occupational qualification). Yet social media sites may contain a lot of additional information, from political and religious beliefs to everyday behaviours, that is irrelevant to the job.

Some of the most common red flags identified by recruiters on social media sites are not legal to use in hiring decisions. 29 per cent of business decision makers say online political views/activity would stop someone getting hired (definitely not legal), and 26 per cent said that having too many photos of themselves on a social media profile could be disqualifying (certainly not a bona fide occupational qualification).

In the 2000s and early 2010s, when some companies were far more tech-savvy than legislators, there was a lot more legal wriggle room to use social media profiles in the job screening process. Now that legislation is trying to catch up to the technology, employers must be more cautious about using social media data in the selection process. If you are going to use social media profiles to screen job candidates, here are some guidelines:

- The guidelines on discrimination and fair hiring practice all apply to social media in the candidate screening process.

- Only data that is relevant to the role can and should be evaluated in the screening process. This includes qualifications, experience, education and factors directly relevant to the job.

- Any personal data collected should be absolutely necessary to the hiring process, and no excessive or irrelevant data should be collected (this can be very challenging to disaggregate from a personal social media profile).

- Social media searches should look for specific, predefined information or criteria and not be a general trawling exercise.

- Reasonable steps should be taken to verify the accuracy of any information.

- Distinguish between social media used for personal vs professional purposes. For example, a LinkedIn profile is typically used for professional purposes, while Facebook is typically used for personal purposes.

- Professional information in the public domain can be used. For example, work they have published, information from professional or trade bodies, and information published from past employers on a public website or social media platform.

- Applicants must be advised of the screening beforehand and provide informed consent for their personal information to be used.

- Applicants should receive the opportunity to respond to any negative or adverse findings that arise from a social media search, and their response should be considered in the decision-making process.

Conclusion

As social media becomes more and more common and easily accessible by anyone, people tend to become more restrictive in their privacy settings.[4] The more information that people post publicly on social media, the more individuals, organizations and computer programs will comb through that data for their own purposes. This understandably has a chilling effect on people's willingness to share their data publicly.

Highly effective analytics can be a victim of their own success. Once people's data can be analysed to make predictions about factors such as personality and behaviour (especially commercial behaviour), many people will become more careful and restrictive about sharing their information. There is good evidence to suggest social media companies and even search engines can go beyond just predicting behaviour to actually influencing it, in everything from shopping decisions to seeking mental health support.[5,6]

The consequence of this is that companies that abuse their access to personal data will make people more cautious about sharing it in the future. This has the potential to erode trust in all businesses, and make it more challenging even for those who operate ethically and legally.

The battle between privacy and access to information online will continue to be a dynamic process for both users and those who employ analytics, as people's behaviour and approach to social media adapt to a continually-evolving landscape. It also means that companies will continue to adapt with social media, its users and in the regulatory landscape.

Notes

1 Social media use in 2018: www.pewinternet.org/2018/03/01/social-media-use-in-2018/ (archived at https://perma.cc/53S4-WJ3W)

2 Can your social media profile kill your job prospects? www.bbc.co.uk/news/business-42621920 (archived at https://perma.cc/8TRA-28DV)

3 Disgracebook: One in five employers have turned down a candidate because of social media: https://yougov.co.uk/topics/politics/articles-reports/2017/04/10/disgracebook-one-five-employers-have-turned-down-c (archived at https://perma.cc/W9B5-CSMC)

4 MacRae, I, and Furnham, A (2018) *High Potential: How to spot, manage and develop talented people at work*, Bloomsbury, London

5 I used Google Ads for social engineering It worked: www.nytimes.com/2019/07/07/opinion/google-ads.html (archived at https://perma.cc/ZRX5-5ALT)

6 Preoţiuc-Pietro, D *et al* (2015) Studying user income through language, behaviour and affect in social media, *PLoS ONE*, 10 (**9**)

SOCIAL MEDIA IS JUST FOR TALKING TO CUSTOMERS

The story of Facebook shows how a reputation can make it much easier or much harder to attract and keep top talent. A company's reputation and public perception drastically affects how appealing the company is to prospective employees.

Introduction

Some fast-growing organizations struggle more to find new employees than customers. The war for talent has moved online, and social media has become a battleground in finding top talent.

According to a 2017 report by LinkedIn, differentiating yourself from the competition is essential for companies that want to attract the best employees – with more than half of respondents saying that the biggest challenge they face in recruiting is competition for talent.[1]

The majority of recruiting budgets still go towards traditional tactics like job boards (30 per cent) and recruitment agency costs (23 per cent), but social media provides a competitive advantage to companies that are trying to differentiate themselves.

In the previous chapter, we advised caution when collecting information about prospective employees, and using that information to screen job candidates. However, organizations have far more options when it comes to sharing their own information, and how they choose to communicate with current and prospective employees.

We could write an entire chapter on attracting employees through social media, or even a whole book on communicating brand identity through social media platforms. However, it's not that complicated. People want to work for companies they like. People want to work for companies that provide good pay, perks and benefits. People want to feel good about what the company they work for does.

Some more adept companies have used their corporate social media presence to make their company more attractive to prospective employees. Attracting good people means convincing them that your company is a desirable place to work – and social media can be a powerful way to do this.

The rise and fall of Facebook

Facebook is one of the world's most talked-about companies, and has one of the largest market capitalizations in the world. In its early days it was seen as an attractive and lucrative place to work, a magnet for top young talent. As it grew to become a dominant brand, Facebook embraced Silicon Valley's long tradition of offering extravagant perks to employees, from gourmet cafeterias to lucrative salaries.[2] They carved out the corpse of the defunct Sun Microsystems building in Menlo, California, then built a sprawling new open-plan building next door. Architecture writer Allison Arieff described it in the *New York Times* as: 'a 420,000-square-foot, single-story warehouse topped with a garden'.[3] Lovely.

Facebook was competing, quite successfully, with Google for the top talent in tech. High-profile people such as Google Maps co-founder Lars Rasmussen were jumping ship for Facebook, saying in 2010: 'It feels to me that Facebook may be a sort of once-in-a-decade type company.'[4]

In recent years, however, Facebook's appeal has been waning, with a series of scandals and PR disasters making it seem like a decidedly less appealing place for employees. What with privacy and data protection scandals, accusations of discrimination within the company and facilitating discrimination for other companies as well as accusations of being a playground for extremists of all stripes, Facebook is quickly losing its reputation as a great place to work that has a positive impact on the world.[5,6,7,8,9]

The story of Facebook shows how a reputation can make it much easier or much harder to attract and keep top talent. Now that Facebook's reputation as an employer is on the decline, other companies have found that it is the perfect place to poach top talent from.[10] In the wake of scandals, as of December 2018 only 35–55 per cent of new graduates from top US universities accepted full-time job offers from Facebook, down from 85 per cent in the 2017–2018 school year.[11]

A company's reputation and public perception drastically affects how appealing the company is to prospective employees. The tech sector is a prime example because high-performing, highly competitive companies battle for the top talent. The rise and fall of public opinion surrounding a company is a perfect example of how opinion can be shaped on social media.

The risk of the blue tick demographic

There is another potential risk when using data from social media, especially if that is the company's only source of data.

One of the advantages of social networks is that a large number of users post their thoughts publicly online. In fact, some companies make great use of this Big Data to analyse general trends in consumer behavior and public opinion. This kind of analysis can reveal at how Twitter users feel about a certain brand, person or idea at a single point in time or over time. It's an expansion of the old political focus group, where a pre-selected demographic rate their feelings about a political speech, for example. It can give specific insight into whether people feel positively or negatively, and why.

The problem is the same that any knowledgeable researcher encounters: is this sample group representative of the wider population as a whole, or the group of people they are interested in? If you pull a group of people out of a fast food restaurant, a supermarket, a social club or a pub, you cannot be sure that they are representative of the entire population. It may be that there are certain traits, characteristics, interests or other factors that bring people together, and these are often factors that influence opinions.

The same is true of social media sites and can be especially true of those who vociferously share their opinions about a certain topic on social media.

Research indicates that social media users are in fact not representative of the general population. In the US, for example, Twitter users tend to be younger, have more post-secondary educational qualifications, have higher incomes and are more liberal than the general population.[12]

And even among those users, there are differences. Most people barely say anything online, while 10 per cent of users generate 80 per cent of all tweets. These prolific tweeters are different from the overall Twitter user base, and even further from the population average, being much more likely to be women, and to post about political subjects.

Social media platforms also differ between themselves, as discussed in Chapter 3. According to 2017 UK research by Mellon and Prosser, users of both platforms have a significantly different demographic profile to the general population, and to each other.[13] In Britain, social media users tend to be younger, more educated and report being more interested in politics (but are less likely to vote) than the general population. However, the research showed that the political differences were better explained by the demographics than by social media use.

We've discussed in other chapters (3, 16, 26 and 28) how different social platforms have different purposes, and are used in different ways. Remember that no platform is completely representative of the population, and each has their own quirks and sub-cultures. While these platforms can be extraordinarily useful for reaching their user base, do not assume that a social media platform is automatically a good gauge of general trends, or of the opinions of all people.

Conclusion

Social media provides an expansive source of information and the opportunity to connect with potential employees as well as customers or clients. There is a lot to be learned about people and their behaviour on social media that organizations, recruiters and hiring managers will find very useful.

However, it is necessary to be cautious about what kind of information you are accessing about people online. Ethical hiring practice as well as employment law is evolving with social media, so if businesses are going to use data they collect about people online, they must make sure they follow both ethical and legal guidelines for doing so.

Businesses, as well as users, are becoming savvier and more sophisticated in their use of social media, as concerns about security and privacy are on the increase. This is not likely to fade in the near future, and businesses who choose to use unethical or illegal practices run the serious risk of legal challenges as well as public opinion backlash.

Notes

1   Global recruiting trends 2017: What you need to know about the state of talent acquisition: https://business.linkedin.com/talent-solutions/cx/2016/10/global-recruiting-trends-2017 (archived at https://perma.cc/2NY7-LS8Q)

2   With high-end meal perks, Facebook keeps up Valley tradition: www.nytimes.com/2009/12/25/us/25sfcafeteria.html (archived at https://perma.cc/D7RM-G4GR)

3   Facebook plays it safe: https://opinionator.blogs.nytimes.com/2012/08/31/facebook-plays-it-safe/ (archived at https://perma.cc/F27R-BPMA)

4   Why I quit Google to join Facebook: Lars Rasmussen: www.smh.com.au/technology/why-i-quit-google-to-join-facebook-lars-rasmussen-20101101-1799q.html (archived at https://perma.cc/5857-L6K3)

5   Cambridge Analytica and Facebook: The scandal and the fallout so far: www.nytimes.com/2018/04/04/us/politics/cambridge-analytica-scandal-fallout.html (archived at https://perma.cc/2QGG-76WL)

6   Facebook employee blasts 'black people problem' at social network: www.telegraph.co.uk/technology/2018/11/27/facebook-employee-blasts-climate-racial-discrimination/ (archived at https://perma.cc/HU47-6CV8)

7   Facebook accused of allowing bias against women in job ads: www.nytimes.com/2018/09/18/business/economy/facebook-job-ads.html (archived at https://perma.cc/69RC-LLMA)

8   Facebook 'auto-generated' extremist video: www.bbc.co.uk/news/technology-48217827 (archived at https://perma.cc/RF2M-P42U)

9   Facebook accused of introducing extremists to one another through 'suggested friends' feature: www.telegraph.co.uk/news/2018/05/05/facebook-accused-introducing-extremists-one-another-suggested (archived at https://perma.cc/FT3D-F5ZN)

10 Health and education start-ups say recruiting has gotten easier in wake of Facebook, Google scandals: www.cnbc.com/2019/04/18/facebook-google-scandals-ease-recruiting-for-health-start-ups.html (archived at https://perma.cc/J4FF-AEFR)

11 Facebook has struggled to hire talent since the Cambridge Analytica scandal, according to recruiters who worked there: www.cnbc.com/2019/05/16/facebook-has-struggled-to-recruit-since-cambridge-analytica-scandal.html (archived at https://perma.cc/TY8V-ZZN5)

12 Sizing up Twitter users: www.pewinternet.org/2019/04/24/sizing-up-twitter-users (archived at https://perma.cc/2FXX-Z4CC)

13 Mellon, J and Prosser, C (2017) Twitter and Facebook are not representative of the general population: Political attitudes and demographics of British social media users, *Research & Politics*, 4 (3)

BEING ACTIVE ON SOCIAL MEDIA LETS ME CONTROL MY DIGITAL FOOTPRINT

Being active online does help you control your active digital footprint, but it's also important to understand how, when, where and why companies are collecting data about you.

Introduction

Everything someone does online leaves some sort of trace. Every website visited, every transaction, social media post or interaction leaves a trail. This is a fact of digital life, and it's impossible to avoid, but it can be managed. It's very important to understand how this works and to know what kind of trail you are leaving online.

Everything company or individual does online leaves a trace, and many companies use these traces of people's online behaviour to target customers. Much of the tracking revolves around identifying people's general patterns of behaviour, desires and opinions online in order to sell them products or services.

Your digital footprint is made up of many different traces of online activity. Posted photos and comments on social media are often among the more visible traces. But everything from shopping online to visiting news and media websites, making Skype calls or sending emails can leave different records.

One of the advantages of actively managing your online presence is that you can influence the form of information that is available about you online. For example, in Chapter 15 we talked about responding to criticism online. In this case, providing channels for people to make complaints and resolve disputes will help to mitigate the negative discussions about a business or a brand on other channels.

The same can be true for individuals. As we discussed in the previous two chapters, individuals can actively manage the information that is available about themselves online. This means that when a person actively manages and curates this information, choosing the content and the channels, they can make sure they can be in control of their digital footprint.

> **Active footprints** are traces you deliberately leave online. This is information associated with you or your computer, or an online account where you post or publish information.
>
> **Passive footprints** are traces that you leave behind online without intending to do so, and sometimes without even knowing that you are leaving a trace. This is information is collected automatically through the course of your online activities.

Generally, it is advisable for everyone to actively manage their digital footprint. And it is especially important for managing professional and corporate reputations. Employers may look for digital footprints of prospective hires. Having a messy footprint can cost people jobs, and damage professional or corporate reputations.

There are great opportunities as well as risks with digital footprints. Having a well-managed footprint can be a great tool for managing professional or corporate reputation. Social media sites in particular let you choose what information you choose to share online and what is publicly available. A strong and positive professional digital footprint can, and often does, attract job offers, recruiters and positive interaction online.

For more information about digital footprints and similar resources, the Internet Society Foundation has some great guides and tutorials.[1]

A case study: The author's digital footprint

To explain the situation, we decided to do some digging into my digital footprint. If you were to look at my digital footprint, you could find a lot of information just by typing 'Ian MacRae' into a search engine. There's more than one 'Ian MacRae', so by adding a keyword like 'psychologist', 'personality', 'leadership' or 'high potential' you would get more accurate results. You'd probably find my social media profiles, links to books and articles I've written, relevant news stories and media appearances. With a bit of digging you might be able to find a bit more. However, that active digital footprint only scratches the surface of my overall digital footprint.

Every company I work with or have an account with tracks information about me that makes up a small proportion of my overall digital footprint. Social media companies have a lot more information about me than is publicly available. Utility providers, airlines, banks, department stores all have information about me and my relationship with them. All of the apps I use, the emails I send, loyalty cards that I swipe and things that I buy online contribute to that footprint.

How much of that information can I track down? It turns out that because of EU General Data Protection Regulation (GDPR) I can get access to all of the personal data every company collects about me. So, I decided to do just that. I put together a list of 100 companies that would have personal data about me (the total list would be longer, but I restricted the search to more frequently used and more recent accounts). The process was relatively easy, although extremely time-consuming.

All companies that fall within European Union jurisdictions are required by GDPR to have a process to provide people with copies of their personal data if requested. Companies have one month to complete the request, where they must provide all of the personal data they store about an individual. This data can be anything from a few lines of text to thousands of pages, or vast spreadsheets of data.

Overall, most companies were quick, responsive and friendly. 93 per cent of the companies did provide me with copies of my personal data, and one of the companies that didn't respond went bust shortly after my request, so would not be expected to complete it.

Results

Based on the results of the GDPR requests, I found I could categorize companies into three general trends in their data collection activities. Where companies did not respond (including Virgin Media, NowTV and Principal Hotel Group) I assumed that the data collection they describe on their privacy policy was accurate:

3 Very minimal data collection. The majority of companies (72 per cent) actually collected and stored surprisingly little personal data. Beginning this process, I was expecting to make unpleasant discoveries about the volume and scale of data collected by the majority of companies. But I was pleasantly surprised to find that many of the companies such as retail stores, train companies, some loyalty card providers and even mobile phone applications were only collecting and storing minimal personal data. Most retail and department stores, for example, only stored my purchase history and basic personal details like name and contact details.

4 Customer profiling in line with business. A smaller segment of companies (19 per cent) had more detailed personal information, or more detailed consumer profiles. These were companies such as supermarkets and some loyalty cards (Nectar) airlines, video games companies and financial institutions. While these companies did store more personal information, it was an entirely reasonable amount of data and in some cases data that would be covered by other regulatory requirements. For example, it's not unreasonable to expect that your bank or credit card company would have information about your personal finances, or that an airline would have copies of your passenger logs from flights with that airline. Streaming websites stored viewing preferences, utility companies had usage history and details, along with communication logs.

5 Expansive data collection. A much smaller proportion (9 per cent) of the companies collected and stored vast amounts of personal data about me. The usual suspects had a disproportionate amount of personal data: Google, Amazon, Apple, Facebook and Twitter. Although Virgin Media did not send me my data after multiple requests and complaints, being an internet service provider (ISP) they certainly fall into this category. This small minority of companies stored more than 99 per cent of the personal data about me.

It's not entirely unreasonable that social media companies would have huge amounts of data, because the purpose of social media companies is to store personal information and communication online. Providing a digital communications platform involves collecting and storing huge amounts of data is the business model, and necessary for the service they provide. The same is true for internet service providers, who are required by law to store customer's internet records for a year. On the surface, this is not necessarily a problem. However, one of the major concerns is when they start collecting data that is not necessary or collecting data without informed consent.

Interestingly, because I use the privacy and security tools that will be discussed in Chapter 25, there were large amounts of inaccurate data. The companies where I left a much larger, passive footprint had more inaccuracies in their data. That's because the privacy tools prevent these companies from automatically collecting accurate personal data such as my location. For example, Twitter had my device location and time zone set as 'Arizona' and my Google location history had fairly extensive location history in Florida (I have never been to Arizona or Florida).

As greater numbers of people use these fairly cheap and simple privacy tools (see Chapter 25), it becomes much more difficult for these companies that collect vast amounts of data to automatically hoover up detailed personal data from people.

Very personal data

Companies and applications that collect the most amount of data are also the companies that run the risk of collecting data that is too personal. It is easy to forget how significant this data collection is when it happens passively. For example, Google collects detailed location history when you use products like Google Maps. This can be a convenient tool for day-to-day use, but when the data is compiled over the years it provides a surprising level of insight into someone's individual behaviour.

For example, Figure 24.1 below shows a map based on my Google location history. The map is shaded based on locations Google has recorded in my location history. While I have displayed the map as country-level data, it is possible to view this location history in much greater detail. It is recorded as specific geographic coordinates and times, so the data is available minute-by-minute and street-by-street. It even estimates how you are travelling (eg 'on foot', 'in vehicle' or 'on bicycle'). My Google location history had over 1 million lines of data about me (1,048,575), but if you regularly use additional location-based products like Fitbit, this amount of data will be substantially higher.

Figure 24.1 Google user location history example

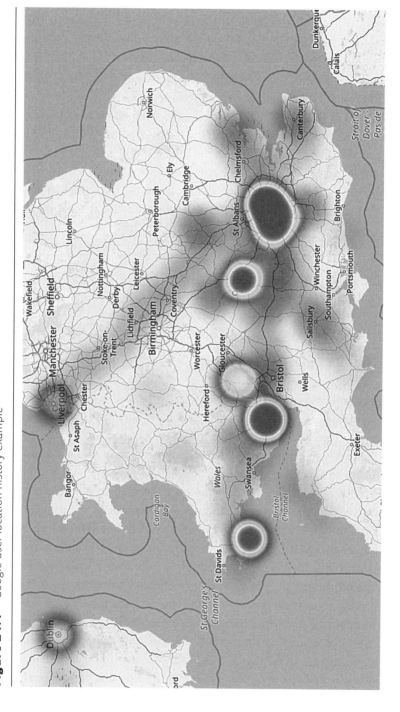

A full, but fragmented picture

Starting this process, I was quite worried about how much personal data I would find about myself. After seeing the results, it was clear that the majority of companies or organizations only collect minimal personal data, largely in line with the basic and necessary information I would expect them to have such as previous transactions, communication history and marketing preferences.

Putting all of the information together from different companies, there was a substantial amount of data that could be combined to create a very detailed look into my daily life, personal behaviour, consumer preferences, spending patterns and activity. However, since most of the data was scattered between many different companies, the personal data from 91 per cent of the more modest data collectors did not reveal very much about me taken separately. But if you put all the data together, you could likely deduce my exercise schedule, eating habits and even sleep habits. You could add in my work calendars, contacts, online communication, household energy use, what films and television I watch, and much more.

However, this data was mostly fragmented. Except for the larger data collectors, the majority of companies only had a small amount of personal data that was not particularly concerning or unreasonable in scale. Supermarkets can be expected to understand your food shopping habits, airlines to have your flight history, your gym to have your activity history, and your bank should know where you are spending your money and how much you make.

I did have three areas of concern:

- Social media and technology companies collect a vast amount of data automatically, and in many cases, this is difficult or impossible to control. Most smartphones and applications are designed to automatically share personal data. This means that location data, like that shown in Figure 24.1, is probably available for most people who regularly use a smartphone. For anyone that uses their phone to track things like their exercise, sleep schedule or food intake, the data is likely to be even more comprehensive. Remember what we said in previous chapters, if the product or service is free, then you are probably not the customer: your data is the product.

- The second major concern was that my internet service provider Virgin Media would not provide me with my personal data. After numerous phone calls, requests, complaints, emails and even a complaint to the regulator, over the course of 183 days, at the time of writing they still have not provided me with the data they store about me (they are required to provide it on request within one month). One of the biggest red flags in privacy and data protection is when companies fail to comply with regulation, and the failure of a company that collects a large amount to comply with the GDPR rules raises significant questions and concerns.

- The third area that is important to note that I generally avoid smartphone applications that collect unnecessary amounts of personal data, and have added security applications on my smartphone to minimize the amount of data that is collected without my consent. Social media smartphone applications are terrible offenders in this area. Mobile games often hoover up unnecessary data and are a significant privacy concern.[2,3,4,5] There are significant concerns around newer and emerging applications such as those that swap, change or enhance people's faces: concerns that in the longer term these will be used for facial recognition or developing deepfake technology.[6] But I have not included these, because I don't use them.

Conclusion

Being active online does help you control your active digital footprint, but it's also important to understand how, when, where and why companies are collecting data about you, particularly the large tech and social media companies. The more knowledgeable you are about what kind of digital footprints you are leaving, the better able you will be to manage and shape the trail of data you leave online.

This is very important for individuals and businesses to understand. For businesses, it can shape and change the way people talk about, and interact with, the business. For individuals, your digital footprint will affect everything from your employment prospects and credit rating to the type and content of news, media and advertising you are presented with.

One of the more optimistic conclusions of this chapter is that most companies in the UK appear to be in line with privacy and data collection recommendations. Banks, supermarkets, airlines, train companies, and retail stores mostly appear to be acting fairly and responsibly with people's personal data. If you are concerned with data protection and privacy, there are a relatively small number of companies that collect the vast majority of personal data.

It's difficult to avoid leaving a digital footprints if you spend any amount of time online, but if you understand the process and have an awareness of the data that is being collected, you can be a more active participant in shaping your experience.

Notes

1 Your Digital Footprint Matters: www.internetsociety.org/tutorials/your-digital-footprint-matters (archived at https://perma.cc/BQ5U-CA56)

2 How smartphone apps track users and share data: https://ig.ft.com/mobile-app-data-trackers (archived at https://perma.cc/U4N8-Y7HM)

3 Data privacy and security: Why mobile apps are the new weak link: www.infosecurity-magazine.com/next-gen-infosec/privacy-mobile-apps-weak-link-1-1 (archived at https://perma.cc/D9UW-24LX)

4 How game apps that captivate kids have been collecting their data: www.nytimes.com/interactive/2018/09/12/technology/kids-apps-data-privacy-google-twitter.html (archived at https://perma.cc/D9Z5-96MQ)

5 That game on your phone may be tracking what you're watching on TV: www.nytimes.com/2017/12/28/business/media/alphonso-app-tracking.html (archived at https://perma.cc/CG7Z-XRNJ)

6 China's red-hot face-swapping app provokes privacy concern: www.bloomberg.com/news/articles/2019-09-02/china-s-red-hot-face-swapping-app-provokes-privacy-concern (archived at https://perma.cc/6CAB-PEN4)

SOCIAL NETWORKS WILL PROTECT MY DATA

It is still fairly safe to assume that any company, even those with the most sophisticated cybersecurity countermeasures, will suffer from accidental leaks, hacks or technical problems at some point in time.

Introduction

In the previous chapter, we discussed the vast amount of personal data that companies are collecting online. It is a relatively small handful of companies that collect the majority of this, whereas most collect only the most basic personal data they need to provide services.

So how much can you trust these tech behemoths with your data? Should you trust the privacy and security measures of the likes of Facebook, Instagram, Twitter, LinkedIn and TikTok to protect your personal data? Or should you be taking additional steps to protect your own information?

Every year companies lose people's data, and seem to break records with every new breach.[1,2] Major companies such as British Airways, Deloitte, Hilton Hotels, Heathrow Airport, Sony Pictures, Facebook, Adobe, Equifax, JP Morgan Chase and the US Postal Service have all suffered data breaches. In April 2019, security consultants IT Governance reported that over 1.34

billion electronic records had been breached.[3] Companies are not always forthcoming about breaches either – it took Yahoo four years to acknowledge that a 2013 beach affected all 3 billion of their users.

Let's assume that all social media companies are completely committed to data protection, security and privacy. It's up to you whether or not you think that is a safe assumption. But even operating on that assumption, it is still fairly safe to assume that any company, even those with the most sophisticated cybersecurity countermeasures, will suffer from accidental leaks, hacks or technical problems at some point in time.[4]

Fortunately, the tools and techniques for keeping yourself and your data safe online are relatively cheap, accessible and easy to use. We outline some of the best options below, and highly recommend using these, if you do not already.

Data protection tools and techniques

Regular software updates

This is one of the easiest and most important steps to keeping your devices safe. Make sure to regularly update the software on your devices. In many cases, and on most new devices, this is done automatically.

Keeping your software updated protects your devices from known viruses and potential problems. It won't protect against every threat, but it is an important first step. Many of the data breaches of companies and even governmental departments have resulted from vulnerabilities in out-of-date software.

Antivirus software

Your device will include some security elements, and keeping the software updated as mentioned in the previous point will help to keep your devices secure. However, dedicated antivirus software can help to keep your devices protected much more effectively than the manufacturer of the device you are using. They tend to offer better protection by scanning files on your device that could be harmful, blocking potentially malicious websites.

There are plenty of companies offering relatively inexpensive and user-friendly antivirus software. Articles in magazines such as *TechRadar* or *PCMag* provide useful lists of recommended antivirus software for different devices.

Private browsing

Private browsing is one of the most basic features for limiting the amount of personal data you share while online. Most browsers come with a built-in 'private', or 'incognito' feature.

When you're in a private browsing window, you computer does not store your own search history, files you've downloaded, or information you are accessing online. Essentially, it means your computer forgets everything you did during the private browsing session after you close the window. What it does not do is stop anyone else from collecting your data. The searches you make in a search engine can still be stored by the activity of other applications, and often will be.

This makes private browsing a fairly limited way to reduce what personal information you share, but it does mean less data is stored on your own device.

Password managers

If you had to take only one simple step to protect your privacy and security online, using a password manager should it. If you take none of the other advice in this chapter, start using a password manager.

One of the biggest security threats online is reusing the same email address or username and password across many different sites. Most people know they shouldn't do this, but do it anyway. Every year when lists of the most popular passwords are published, there is little change. Up until recently, the most common password was 'password', although it is now in second place, and an astounding number of people still choose easy-to-crack variants such as '123456', 'query', 'admin', 'abc123' or 'iloveyou'. Topical passwords are always popular too, such as 'solo', 'dragon', 'donald' and 'batman'.

Again, please do not do this. If you see your password above, change it today. Don't make your password your surname, the name of your child or the street you live on. Just adding a 1 or ! to the end when required is not great either, even though many people do it.

Invest in a password manager. There are plenty of very good, highly secure companies that offer this, including Lastpass or 1Password. A password manager will generate random passwords for each of the different sites you use, and store this information securely. They are easy to use, and typically come with apps for your computer and phone that will autocomplete your usernames and passwords for all of your different logins.

Of course, you should have one master password to log in to the password manager that is both secure (not 123456), relatively easy to remember and not used anywhere else. Usernames and passwords get hacked, leaked or guessed all the time. Getting used to using a password manager may take a bit of time, but it is one of the quickest and most effective way to protect yourself and your data online.

Identifying data breaches

Companies are not always quick to disclose when they have lost people's data. Although they should immediately inform everything who has been affected, the reality is that sometimes the people who could be the most affected are the last to find out.

If your username and password has been stolen from a website you use, the best thing to do is immediately change that password, and make sure you also change it anywhere else you may have used it.

There's a very good free service that alerts you if there have been any data breaches associated with your email account called Have I Been Pwned?[5] You can subscribe using your email address to be alerted if and when that email address is associated with any data leaks or breaches. It doesn't require any personal information other than your email address, which most people feel comfortable handing out. Avoid similar services that ask for your password or other sensitive information.

This is another very quick and easy step you can take to protect your personal information online.

Virtual Private Networks

Typically, when you are online, most of your activity will be connected with you through your Internet Service Protocol (ISP) address. This means that every website you visit gets a number to identify you, that connects you to your internet service provider and physical location. Many companies will track your activity online (your internet provider keeps a log of every website you have visited over the last year). Social media sites are among the worst offenders, tracking much of your online activity even when you are not on their site.

A Virtual Private Network (VPN) essentially uses a highly encrypted connection and puts all of the information you are sending into a black box. About 25 per cent of internet users now connect through a VPN.[6]

The privacy and security benefits of this should be obvious. It restricts external parties or companies from being able to 'listen in' on your online activity. Whenever you are sending or receiving information, especially related to business activities, client or customer data, private communications, or confidential documents, it is sent privately and securely.

Again, let's assume that the companies that are keeping track of your history are doing their very best to protect your privacy and security, and that your internet service provider and social media companies are not going to use your data for unethical purposes. There is still the risk of all of that data being released publicly in a hack or a leak. Internet service providers have lost people's personal data before, and it will almost certainly happen again. Most people would likely be quite unhappy to see a list of every single website they had accessed in the previous 12 months. By putting it all in that secure VPN black box, it keeps your personal or private data secure and private.

There are plenty of companies that offer VPN services quite inexpensively. There are some free options, but these are usually too slow to be practical.

Two-factor authentication

More and more companies that hold important data or have access to financial accounts are moving to two-factor authentication. Most banks now use a variety of two-factor authentication methods to keep their customers' accounts more secure. Methods vary, but it essentially means that two different security steps are required to access an account. This can include email, text or phone call verification as well as a password, making it more difficult for unauthorized users to access people's accounts.

As well as financial accounts, it is advisable to have two-factor authentication on any accounts that hold personal, sensitive or security information, or which themselves could be used to reset a lost password or as a second factor in authentication, such as email accounts.

Physical authentication devices

Physical authentication is a type of authentication that requires a material (not digital) security step. It can be a device that creates a numerical or visual code that can be used to log in to accounts, or one which has a smart chip that needs to be connected to another device as a security measure. These are typically plugged into a USB or audio port, but can also use a wireless connection.

Essentially, these protect devices or accounts by making sure no one can access these without the physical token. This can take a bit longer to set up, and can cause problems if you misplace the physical token. It does, however, offer a much stronger level of security for accounts that are important to keep secure.

Conclusion

All of this might sound like a bit of an annoyance – more things to think about when you're online, making everything just a little bit more complicated. Of course, you don't have to do it, just like you don't have to lock your doors or turn the oven off when you leave the house. But it is strongly advised you do so to prevent serious problems in the future.

All of these steps are relatively easy to take, most are inexpensive and some are completely free. Even taking a few small steps like keeping your software updated and using strong, unique passwords on your accounts will go a long way in protecting your security or your company's security online.

Most people are completely reliant on digital infrastructure, and we often do not realize how embedded it is in our everyday lives until something goes wrong. Taking a few extra steps to protect yourself and your company online can go a long way. Organizations should also take steps to teach their employees about the importance of staying secure online as more and more business communications and processes move into digital spaces.

Notes

1 Data breaches keep happening. So why don't you do something? www.nytimes. com/2018/08/01/technology/data-breaches.html (archived at https://perma.cc/ E4CP-PFHB)

2 Millions of Facebook user records exposed in data breach: www.telegraph. co.uk/technology/2019/04/03/millions-facebook-user-records-exposed-data-breach (archived at https://perma.cc/7MLN-VXA7)

3 List of data breaches and cyber attacks in April 2019 – 134 billion records leaked: www.itgovernance.co.uk/blog/list-of-data-breaches-and-cyber-attacks-in-april-2019-1-34-billion-records-leaked (archived at https://perma.cc/Q3CR-HHT7)

4 Americans and cybersecurity: www.pewinternet.org/2017/01/26/americans-and-cybersecurity (archived at https://perma.cc/6649-G2RC)

5 Have I Been Pwned? https://haveibeenpwned.com (archived at https://perma.cc/ AYG8-HK6M)

6 VPN Usage around the world in 2018: https://blog.globalwebindex.com/ chart-of-the-day/vpn-usage-2018 (archived at https://perma.cc/NN8M-FR8M)

MYTH
26

SOCIAL MEDIA IS THE BEST SOURCE OF INFORMATION

One of the challenges of having such vast quantities of information easily available is that more choice does not always lead to better decision-making.

Introduction

There's something strange or serious going on nearby, and you want to find out what it is. Perhaps it's extra police activity, or a local event. No one you know knows about it, and it has not been reported in the news. The only information you have is a specific time and location – so what's the best way to find out what is going on?

You would either ask someone who is involved (not always practical or reasonable), or check social media. If something notable is happening in a populated area, there are probably other people talking about it on Twitter. News travels fast on social networks, and sometimes it is the fastest and easiest way to get information or start a discussion, perhaps by following a trusted source such as a journalist or researcher.

There is, of course, fake news, false information and propaganda all over social media (as we discuss in detail in Chapter 14). This means getting that finding accurate information on social media can be a bit of a filtering exercise. But, as we discuss in Chapter 28, it is certainly possible to shape your own social media environment to be dominated by trustworthy and reliable sources of information.

In fact, as it turns out, the vast majority of people are sceptics when it comes to information on social media.

Finding trusted sources

The main point of this chapter is that social media can be an excellent source of information – when the source is credible.

Research from the Media Insight Project in 2016 found that most social media users are relatively savvy about filtering out misinformation on the networks and finding trusted sources.[1] This varies by platform, but only 12 per cent of people say they have a great deal of trust in information on Facebook, and even on the most trusted platform, LinkedIn, only 23 per cent of people had a great deal of trust in news they encountered there.

In 2017, the same body conducted an experimental study to investigate how people viewed and interacted with stories based on the publisher and person who shared the story.[2] The exact same story was presented to different people, but attributed to different sources. They found that both trust in the publisher and in the person who shared the story influenced how people saw its credibility.

Social media often has two points of reference for trust, because much of the information is originally posted by one source, then shared by someone else. Both these sources influenced how people viewed the information:

- **Trust in the person who shared the article**. When people see information from a trusted source, they are more likely to believe the article 'got the facts right', and that the information was more well reported or more trustworthy. People are also far more likely to share the article or recommend it to friends when it comes from a trusted source.

- **Trust in the original source**. In the 2017 study, two groups of people were shown an article and told that it came from either a made-up source or the Associated Press. Unsurprisingly, most were more likely to believe that the article was accurate when they believed that it was by the Associated Press. However, those who reported not trusting mainstream news sources were far more likely to believe the article when they thought it came from a publication they hadn't heard of.

The research found that although both the source and the sharer had an effect on how people viewed the information, trust in the sharer was actually more important than trust in the original source. The message is both clear and unsurprising: people are influenced by people they trust. The slightly troubling finding is that people are likely to believe a made-up source over an accurate and credible source they have heard of, but do not trust.

This doesn't entirely answer the question of whether or not social media as a whole is a good source of information. It does show that people are fairly discerning about both the original source of information and the person who is sharing it when they decide whether or not to trust what they see on social media.

One major concern is when people 'trust' unreliable sources. Of course, there are some prominent people and organizations that are less than reliable and honest. Added to this, there are a staggering number of fake accounts on social media. Facebook alone deleted 3 billion fake accounts between October 2018 and March 2019.[3] We discussed fake news and similar phenomena in Chapter 14.

A balanced diet of information

The internet has made information easy, fast and cheap to access for everyone, and it has become more and more widely used by all types of users, from casual searchers to academics.[4] But one of the challenges of having such vast quantities of information easily available is that more choice does not always lead to better decision-making.

When looking for information, people have a tendency to look for the most accessible information source, even if it is not the most accurate. When people have questions about their health, for example, where do most people go first? A doctor? Friends and family? Their taxi driver?

No, the majority of people's first source of information about health and medical problems is the internet.[4,5,6] For health issues from pregnancy to kidney problems, most people choose the internet over a medical professional.

We would highly recommend checking with a doctor before asking Doctor Google, but that does not mean that social media cannot still be a valuable tool. According to a 2011 study, social networks have 'significant potential to sway individuals' attitudes'.[7] The researchers highlighted how important it is that reputable sources post on these networks, given their reach and influence, so that reliable information ends up being disseminated.

And if people are going to check with the internet first for medical advice, they will almost certainly turn to social media for business advice.

In study after study, researchers find that convenience is the most important factor in choosing information sources. However, when you're making business decisions, it is necessary to prioritize accuracy over convenience. Better quality information will lead to better decision-making. We have provided a framework for evaluating information in Chapter 14 on fake news.

It may also be useful to judge sources based on their the amount of time they take to be published. Generally, those which have a longer publication timescale go through a more rigorous and discerning editorial process. As shown in Table 26.1, different information sources have greatly different

Table 26.1   Sources based on publication timescale

Publication timescale	Sources	Content	Intended audience	Written by
Seconds	Social media, blogs, radio, TV	News reporting, quick summary information and commentary	General public or specific interest groups	Anyone
Days	Newspapers, TV, radio	News and commentary	General public	Journalists, subject matter experts
Weeks	Popular magazines	Popular topics for general or specialist audiences	General public	Journalists, subject matter experts
Months	Scholarly journals	Research results and scientific analysis	Academics, specialists, students	Academics, specialists in the field
1+ years	Books	In-depth coverage of a specific topic	General audience, audience with interest in specific topic	Academics, specialists, subject matter experts
5+ years	Reference sources, textbooks	Big-picture, factual information which may include all of the above sources	General audience, audience with interest in specific topic	Specialists, subject matter experts

Adapted from UCF Libraries, The Information Cycle

publication timescales. Information can be posted on social media within seconds, while lengthy and well-researched works can take months or even years to be published.

A well-researched publication that has gone through a rigorous editorial process by a reliable and trustworthy publisher can be regarded as a much better information source. However, there may be overlap between the different sources. This book itself cites a range of sources, from social media and magazines to scientific journals, books and textbooks. To take another example, the quotes at the beginning of each chapter may be regarded as a 'snapshot' of the information within. However, the full text provides much more detail and context than a brief summary.

Another way to evaluate a source is to look at how long it has been available. Books, for example, tend to get lengthier and more in-depth critiques than fleeting social media posts. This can make it easier to evaluate the quality of a source based on the opinions of reputable third parties, as well as the reputation of the author and publisher.

Conclusion

Social media can be a useful source of information, but is not always the best place to get accurate insight. News from your social feeds can be part of a balanced diet of information consumption, but should certainly not be your only source.

This is particularly important for making business decisions. When decision-making has the potential to affect a great deal of staff, customers or profitability, a range of sources should be used to get the best and most accurate information.

Notes

1 A new understanding: What makes people trust and rely on news: www.americanpressinstitute.org/publications/reports/survey-research/trust-news (archived at https://perma.cc/672B-STC4)

2 'Who shared it?': How Americans decide what to trust on social media: www.americanpressinstitute.org/publications/reports/survey-research/trust-social-media (archived at https://perma.cc/8FEG-AVZH)

3 Facebook: Another three billion fake profiles culled: www.bbc.co.uk/news/technology-48380504 (archived at https://perma.cc/7NYE-YE32)

4 Xie, I and Joo, S (2010) Selection of information sources: Accessibility of and familiarity with sources, and types of tasks, *Proceedings of the American Society for Information Science and Technology*, 46 (**1**), pp 1–18

5 Case, D O *et al* (2004) From two-step flow to the internet: the changing array of sources for genetics information seeking, *Journal of the American Society for Information Science and Technology*, 55 (**8**), pp 660–69

6 Lima-Pereira, P, Bermúdez-Tamayo and Jasienska, G (2011) Use of the internet as a source of health information amongst participants of antenatal classes *Journal of Clinical Nursing*, 21 (**3–4**), pp 332–30

7 Sood, A *et al* (2011) YouTube as a source of information on Kidney Stone Disease, *Endourology and Stone*, 77 (**3**), pp 558–62

**MYTH
27**

SOCIAL MEDIA ISN'T THAT INFLUENTIAL

*Not only has social media pervaded our lives as a means
of communication and entertainment, it's also enabled
individuals to become social superstars.*

Introduction

Whether we like it or not, digital has totally pervaded our everyday lives.

We're not just living in a digital age, but so too a 'social media age', in which 98 per cent of digital consumers are social network users, according to the GlobalWebIndex Social Flagship Report.[1]

The latest We Are Social annual research report, which tracks internet and social media usage, identifies that the number of internet users worldwide is 4.388 billion.[2] Comparatively, and contrary to some news reports that social media usage is waning, the number of social media users worldwide is 3.484 billion – up 9 per cent year on year.

As mentioned in Chapter 2, we're spending approximately two hours and 16 minutes of our time on social media channels each day. As outlined in the Social Flagship Report, among the 16- to 24-year-old demographic this is even higher, having just reached three hours a day.

Social media is most certainly no longer new. What started out as a platform to share updates and photos has now been embraced, to some level, by pretty much every demographic, and is fully ingrained into how we connect and communicate. And whether you love them or hate social networks, when it comes to business and commerce, they are becoming increasingly powerful.

Not too many years ago, social media was dismissed as the latest fad, yet adoption and dependency continues to rise. In this chapter, we will explore just how influential social media channels have become.

Social media and consumer influence

According to research from Sprout Social, 74 per cent of shoppers – both business to consumer (B2C) and business to business (B2B) – make buying decisions based on information on social media.[3] Similarly, the PwC 2018 Global Consumer Insights Survey named social media as the most influential channels for inspiring purchases (more so than websites, review sites, direct mail, email, comparison sites, press advertising and many others).[4]

As discussed in Chapter 3, social media is now an integral part of product research, with 40 per cent of people using social media to research new brands or products. In the younger demographic (the 16- to 24-year-olds), according to the Social Flagship Report, social media comes top, overtaking traditional search engines.

The Social Flagship Report further states that a decent proportion of users are swayed by what people say about brands on these platforms, with a quarter of under-35s saying that seeing a brand or product with a lot of 'likes' would encourage them to purchase. Even among the 35- to 44-year-olds, 20 per cent state the same. To back this finding up, according to Sprout Social's research, 45 per cent of global respondents said that online reviews, comments and feedback influence their shopping behaviour.

Take a moment to reflect and consider your own purchasing behaviour and how influenced you are by consumer reviews, for example on sites such as AirBNB, TripAdvisor and Amazon. It's likely that with a quick scroll on your phone, you too have been swayed by the wisdom of the crowd.

And it transpires that what we're looking to purchase also has a bearing on where we turn for influence. A 2015 McKinsey report found that the degree of impact varies depending on what is being purchased.[5] Their study found that for utility products, 15 per cent of respondents reported using social media to assist with their purchase, whereas for other categories such as travel, investment services and over-the-counter drugs from pharmacies, the percentage increased to around 40–50 per cent.

Their study also found a relationship with loyalty – first-time purchasers were 50 per cent more likely to turn to social media for recommendations than a repeat buyer.

Direct sales on social

What's interesting to note is that while there's clear evidence that our purchasing decisions are influenced by social media, social media channels are not yet the preferred choice for making the actual sale.

As reported in the GlobalWebIndex research, social media plays a big role in the buying journey right up to the point of purchase, but the appetite to complete the transaction directly via social media platforms remains low – with many users preferring to switch across to the retail site.

Many efforts are being made to change this by the likes of Instagram, using 'Buy now' buttons and tagging features that enable users to see in-depth product details in a post. Indeed, at the time of writing, Instagram has just announced the launch of a new in-app checkout capability that lets users buy products directly from the Instagram app – aptly named Checkout on Instagram.

Pinterest also has 'Buy now' buttons, and many highly targeted social advertising campaigns have been run across the platforms, encouraging users to buy directly via their site. However, the Social Flagship Report highlights that currently only 12 per cent say that a 'Buy' button on social media encourages them to make a purchase.

Having researched various papers and studies, there's no direct evidence to say why this would be the case, other than force of consumer habit. After all, changing behaviour takes time. Online shopping is now the norm, whereby as little as ten years ago, that simply wasn't the case.

However, the We Are Social report outlines evidence that in China, social media as a direct commerce platform is highly successful. Whether there are inherent cultural differences impacting the general reluctance to buy via social in the West, or other factors at play, it will be interesting to see whether social media moving towards more of an entertainment and shopping function, together with the increased ease of in-app purchasing, will in time move the direct sales needle. Our prediction is that it will.

The influencer marketing industry

Not only has social media pervaded our lives as a means of communication and entertainment, it's also enabled individuals to become social superstars. 'Social influencers' is a term used to describe individuals who have built a significant fan base via social media. And as we explored in more detail in

Chapter 20, fame, once only afforded to popstars, movie stars, sports stars or TV celebrities, is within the reach of 'ordinary' people.

Social media has given a golden opportunity to anyone who wants to build their own brand and influence online. Whether it's arts and crafts, gaming, singing, skateboarding, BMX stunting, comedy or unboxing – effectively, anything goes – charisma and passion chimes with audiences, growing significant engagement.

These often large and highly engaged fan bases have created a whole new influencer marketing industry. Just as we trust our friends and family via social media, so too do we trust these highly engaged strangers.

This type of marketing has become big business, with many huge brands tapping into influencers and their networks to endorse, promote and extend the reach of their product, service or cause.

For example, if an influencer, whether sponsored or not, shares a post speaking favourably about a pair of trainers and tagging the product or including a link, it's likely that those following them will at the very least check out the product – or indeed seek to purchase. According to the Digital Marketing Institute, 49 per cent of consumers follow influencer recommendations, and 40 per cent had purchased something after seeing it on Twitter, YouTube or Instagram.[6]

Putting aside the fact that influencer marketing has had its fair share of bad press, particularly related to consumer trust and fake influencers using social bots to gather fake followers, the Digital Marketing Institute says that by 2020, the influencer marketing industry, worth just £1.5 billion in 2017, is estimated to reach £7.8 billion.

Social media advertising

On the subject of influence, it's worth considering how social media advertising is impacting our purchases and actions. We touch on the effect of targeted advertising and messaging in Chapter 7, and discuss the highly negative impact this can sometimes have (as seen in our examples relating to Cambridge Analytica and the impact on both the US election and the UK's Brexit vote).

There's no denying that advertising on social media has become highly sophisticated. The data insights and real-time tracked consumer behaviours and preferences provide advertisers with granular demographics and insights to effect hyper targeted and relevant messaging.

Figure 27.1 Where social networks impact the user journey

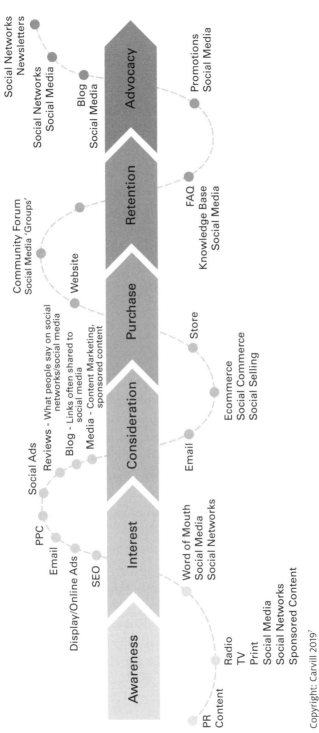

Copyright: Carvill 2019[7]

From a traditional marketing and sales perspective, social media proliferates at every point of the traditional consideration funnel, from awareness all the way through to advocacy.

Adobe's Digital Advertising Survey 2018, looking at digital advertising trends and activity, cites social media as the channel of the future for new customer acquisition, due to its with their mass adoption, share of demographic and association with smartphones.[8]

Social media's relationship with the smartphone is not to be underestimated. As reported in the We Are Social report, 90 per cent of social media activity is executed via mobile – and let's face it, we're all addicted to our mobile phones, which significantly boosts the success of social's hyper-targeted and relevant advertising messages. It's difficult to name any other advertising platform that offers the same level of granular targeting, reach, and the ability to send timely messages directly into the palms of our hands.

Building communities

Beyond using social media to directly sell products or services, organizations are also turning to social networks to build powerful communities.

The increasing use of ad blockers and more consumers generally switching off the noise of traditional push advertising, coupled with the rise of the 'belief-driven buyer', means that more consumers, brands and organizations are harnessing the power of social media to build relationships rather than to advertise.[9] They use it to engage on a more personal level, not only to build loyalty, but to educate their audiences and encourage them to share experiences, support one another and come together to develop change initiatives.

For example, as described in the Global Consumer Insights Survey, Under Armour has developed an online fitness community encouraging their customers to share content across their range of social media, joined by Under Armour athletes such as former number one golfer Jordan Spieth. Patagonia, the outdoor clothing and accessories brand, has built a community around its core brand values aligned with environmental causes – educating customers to consider the environmental impact of their purchases.

Conclusion

It's clear to see how influential social media is becoming to our purchasing behaviour and how we engage with and feel about brands and organizations.

The internet, social media and mobile are inextricably linked – which is having a considerable impact on not only our lives, but also the consumer journey.

Notes

1　Social Flagship Report 2019: www.globalwebindex.com/hubfs/Downloads/ 2019%20Q1%20Social%20Flagship%20Report.pdf (archived at https://perma. cc/64VD-TM5S)

2　Digital in 2019: https://wearesocial.com/global-digital-report-2019 (archived at https://perma.cc/5NLV-ED9J)

3　How Social Media is Influencing Purchase Decisions: https://socialmediaweek. org/blog/2017/05/social-media-influencing-purchase-decisions (archived at https://perma.cc/CLQ7-LJ4A)

4　Global Consumer Insights Survey 2018: Whom Do Customers Really Trust? www.pwc.com/gx/en/retail-consumer/assets/consumer-trust-global-consumer-insights-survey.pdf (archived at https://perma.cc/ENR4-ACGS)

5　Getting a Sharper Picture of Social Media's Influence: www.mckinsey.com/ business-functions/marketing-and-sales/our-insights/getting-a-sharper-picture-of-social-medias-influence (archived at https://perma.cc/3F7E-ULP5)

6　20 Influencer Marketing Statistics that will Surprise You: https:// digitalmarketinginstitute.com/en-gb/blog/20-influencer-marketing-statistics-that-will-surprise-you (archived at https://perma.cc/AQ5C-ABHR)

7　Carvill Creative: www.carvillcreative.co.uk (archived at https://perma.cc/ F453-BHP9)

8　State of Digital Advertising 2018: Adobe Analyses 345B Emails, Website Visits and Video Views: www.forbes.com/sites/johnkoetsier/2018/04/04/state-of-digital-advertising-2018-adobe-analyses-345b-emails-website-visits-and-video-views (archived at https://perma.cc/R9SZ-C4LV)

9　2018 Edelman Earned Brand: Brands Take a Stand: www.edelman.com/sites/g/ files/aatuss191/files/2018-10/2018_Edelman_Earned_Brand_Global_Report.pdf (archived at https://perma.cc/NB6R-6UEV)

SOCIAL MEDIA PRODUCES INFORMATION BUBBLES

The idea that certain individuals or groups are only exposed to self-selected content is nothing new, and certainly not an invention of social media.

Introduction

The internet, and computers, along with social media, have made producing, publishing and distributing content far cheaper than ever before. The reduction in cost and increased accessibility means that a wide range of content has flourished online. This has made it much easier for many with different points of view to find and share a diverse range of information, opinion and content.

One of the advantages of this is it makes it much easier for people to learn about the world and connect with other similar-minded people. Whatever your interests are, the internet and social media opens up access to discussion and sharing. However, this advantage also has the potential to cause problems. It makes it equally easy for people with unsavory, unethical or even illegal interests to connect with each other anywhere in the world.

The question is whether or not, and to what degree, people are exposed to information and opinion from outside their own interest groups. A group of people who are only exposed to a very narrow view of information and opinion are said to exist in a 'filter bubble'.

There is a tendency for bubbles of information and opinion to form on-line, and particularly on social media, as there is in the real world. In this chapter we'll look at issues concerning bubbles, including how isolating they really are, and the role of social media.

The second issue we'll discuss relates to the relevance and importance of bubbles to business. How do companies interact with different bubbles, or groupings of people, online? Is this something that businesses need to take special measures to manage, or is it just a natural phenomenon that emerges from regular social interaction? And, do businesses, departments and teams end up in their own bubble?

To clarify that we're not talking about soap bubbles or a clown, we're going to use the term 'filter bubbles' for the rest of the chapter to describe social groups or environments where only specific types of information or opinion exist, while much is filtered out.

Do filter bubbles exist?

There has been a good deal of scientific research investigating the cause and effects of filter bubbles – and, interestingly, this research goes back at least 70 years. The idea that certain individuals or groups are only exposed to self-selected content is nothing new, and certainly not an invention of social media.

There are two competing theories about the role of social media in creating bubbles. While some researchers such as Iyengar and Hahn suggest the online social media environment creates polarization and the creation of echo chambers,[1] others such as Messing and Westwood believe that the environment of social media actually increases to exposure of alternative viewpoints.[2]

The research shows that there is some evidence on each side of the debate. Certainly, some filtering of information does exist. People do have a tendency to look for information they agree with, and social media algorithms have a tendency to show people content similar to previous content they have seen. However, Messing and Westwood also found that popularity and social endorsements of content are more powerful than ideological affiliation. That is, things that are popular and widely shared tend to get through the bubbles. On social media, it is actually much harder to avoid all dissenting points of view.

There has been very useful recent research conducted on this topic. A study by Flaxman and colleagues in 2016 started by analysing the online behavior of 1.2 million Americans. Then narrowed down their sample group to 50,000 people who met all of the study criteria (including being regular online news consumers).

Their research showed that although people did tend to have moderate preferences towards sources that aligned with their political beliefs, the large majority of users accessed sources across the political divide. Both Republicans and Democrats accessed stories from a range of sources. There was a small amount of bias, but the effect was modest. The large majority of those interested in political news did not appear to exist in a bubble.[3]

There are limitations to the research, partly because the focus was on mainstream news sources, and partly because participants were by definition part of a group that were happy to share their data. However, the general conclusion is that the vast majority of people in their study were not too polarized, and not living entirely in a bubble.

The other implication, though, is that the smaller segments with more extreme views are more likely to exist in a bubble, and their bubbles are likely to be less porous.

How filter bubbles are created

It is not new for people to seek out content, information and opinions that are similar to the beliefs they already hold. Psychologists call this 'confirmation bias'. The phenomenon of confirmation bias was originally described by psychologists in the 1960s to explain a natural tendency in human behavior that has existed throughout history.

Filter bubbles and bias are not new to politics, either. The earliest research on political confirmation bias and filter bubbles goes back to research conducted during the 1940 Presidential election in the US. Democrats were more likely to be exposed to Democratic campaigning, and Republicans were more likely to be exposed to Republican campaigning.[4] Not very surprising, but perhaps comforting to know that filter bubbles are not unique to the online environment.

There are similar examples from other countries where those on the left tend to read left-leaning publications, those on the right side of the political spectrum read right-leaning publications, Catholics read Catholic publications while Protestants read Protestant publications. Research from the Netherlands by Borgesius and colleagues found that this trend goes back through the 20th century.[5]

So confirmation bias is not a phenomenon that has emerged out of the internet and social media. Social media, however, does have the potential to make seeking information congruent with your own worldview very quick and easy. So, the question is worth asking: is social media exacerbating these natural tendencies?

There are two ways that the online environment is a bit different to everyday life. Firstly, a staggeringly wide range of news and opinions is quickly and easily available – so it is much easier for people to create their own online bubbles. Secondly, search engines and social media sites do filter information based on what they think their users might already want to see.

Borgesius *et al* describe these two different ways bubbles can be created:

- **Self-selecting personalization** is when people choose content that aligns with their worldview. This is classic confirmation bias. For example, people with a strong political ideology are likely to read publications that tell them what they want to hear (read how fake news website capitalized on this in Chapter 14). Or, conspiracy theorists may be drawn in deeper to deeply strange belief systems by seeking out information. For example, if you believe the Earth is flat and you search for content that supports that belief online, you will find some.

- **Pre-selected personalization** is when there are filters that go on in the background of search engines, websites and social media. The algorithms dictate what a person sees – typically based on what they have looked at before, their demographics, previous social media activity or other any other data they have left from their footprints online. This happens without the user consenting, or necessarily even knowing that it's happening.

These two types of personalized filter bubbles can feed into each other as well. For example, if you have been searching about 'Flat Earth' theories, your social media accounts will be more likely to show you related pages and adverts. YouTube will start recommending conspiracy theory videos, and Amazon will happily advertise the tinfoil you might need to make your own hat.

If filter bubbles are a natural human phenomenon that could be amplified by social media online, what are the implications for business?

The business implications

Let's look at how filter bubbles can have an impact in a workplace or organization. Within a company, people pre-select their own filter bubbles by choosing to interact with colleagues who work in the same team or department, or people they need to interact with regularly to get their job done. A company's internal social media could also create pre-selected filter bubbles by prioritizing information from certain people within the company that have similar roles and responsibilities.

On the surface, people are likely to have a level of both self-selecting personalization and pre-selected personalization in their social networks by the nature of where they work. Take, for example, the work-based social network LinkedIn. People are more likely to connect with those in similar positions, at the same employer or in a similar sector. Because of that, people are likely to cultivate connections with those who have a similar background and experience to them, and consequently will tend to be exposed to similar content. It is likely that people who work for an oil and gas company, for example, will see very different content than people who work for an environmental charity. This, too, should not be surprising. It is an amplification of what happens naturally in the workplace.

Issues to consider

There are a range of issues, opportunities and risks associated with filter bubbles in social media. These are not necessarily positive or negative, but form a useful framework for discussing the business implications:

- **Polarization.** One of the issues with social media bubbles is that it has the potential to drive people with different opinions further apart and reduce levels of agreement or understanding between groups. For businesses this poses a very obvious opportunity, along with a serious risk. It makes it relatively easy to target a particular group and play upon the attitudes within that group. For example, one political group may have a series of jokes, imagery and memes they use in a humorous context. It may be tempting to use those jokes in a marketing campaign to appear to a certain group. The risk of polarization for businesses is that attempts to appeal to one group could alienate other groups.

- **New gatekeepers and influencers.** The traditional gatekeepers of information and opinion were people like press barons, public censors or state regulators. Now content providers such as app stores, social media websites and search engines are major gatekeepers and influencers. These are the organizations which provide pre-selected personalization.

They are both gatekeepers as well as major advertising companies. Popular companies and users on these platforms have also become major influencers.

- **Concerns about autonomy.** Filter bubbles have the potential to either increase or diminish personal autonomy and independence. Self-selected personalization can increase the breadth of information people have access to. Conversely, some would argue pre-selected personalization reduces personal autonomy when people's options online are limited to a very specific range that has been chosen for them, instead of opening up access.

- **Lack of transparency.** An ongoing concern about pre-selection filter bubbles is that many online giants do not make their algorithms public, and people do not know exactly how they are being influenced. Organizations would be advised to be as transparent as possible about the ways they use and interact with social media. This is discussed in much more detail in Chapters 14, 22 and 23.

- **Social sorting.** Another concern raised about social media is the risks associated with sorting people into different categories. This may create problems, but it is certainly not uncommon or new. In business it's known as market segmentation. The capacity to easily identify and target communications to specific groups or individuals is a fantastically useful for businesses. There are many legitimate and ethical ways to do this, but problems arise when the practices are discriminatory or disadvantage certain groups (for example, targeting job advertisements at a particular demographic group). Recent research has found social media algorithms can introduce significant racial bias into targeted marketing, even when that is not the advertiser's intention.[6] This, like many of the issues raised, is extremely important to consider, because making mistakes (even out of ignorance instead of malice) can create serious ethical, legal and business problems.

Conclusion

Filter bubbles happen, and were a common part of life before social media existed. However, social media may have the capacity to make these bubbles more isolating and insular. It's something to be aware of, but it is not necessarily something that can be changed or needs to be 'fixed'.

The research shows that while there is some polarization that occurs online, the majority of people are exposed to a fairly wide variety of information and opinion. For the majority, there may be a bit of insulation that occurs through self-selection and pre-selection of information. This is relatively similar to the confirmation bias phenomenon, which has existed throughout human history.

There does seem to a be a tendency for those with more extreme views to be more vulnerable to filter bubbles. Their own extreme beliefs combined with social media algorithms can be a quick route to much less porous bubbles – but this is a small segment of the population, not the majority.

Businesses need to be aware that filter bubbles exist to varying degrees. There are advantages to this, because any business strategy relies on a common vision for the organization and the people who work there. Internal use of social media and an online presence can enhance this. Bubbles are also, essentially, market segments, so this makes it easy to target potential customers, clients or employees online.

There are disadvantages too. Companies can become too insular and can easily fall into bubbles where they are disconnected with outside viewpoints. A business being out of touch or unaware will rarely lead to good decision-making or policy.

Notes

1 Iyengar, S and Hahn, K S (2009) Red Media, Blue Media: Evidence of ideological selectivity in media use, *Journal of Communication*, 59, 19–39

2 Messing, S and Westwood, S J (2012) Selective exposure in the age of social media: Endorsements trump partisan source affiliation when selecting news online, *Communication Research*, 41, 1042–63

3 Flaxman, S Goel, S and Rao, J M (2016) Filter bubbles, echo chambers, and online news consumption, *Public Opinion Quarterly*, 80, 298–320

4 Lazarsfeld, P F, Berelson, B and Gaudet, H (1944) *The people's choice: How the voter makes up his mind in a presidential campaign*, Columbia University Press, New York

5 Borgesius, F J Z *et al* (2016) Should we worry about filter bubbles? *Internet Policy Review*, 5 (1)

6 Facebook's ad algorithm discriminates even when it's not told to, study finds: http://nymag.com/intelligencer/2019/04/facebooks-ad-algorithm-is-a-fully-functional-racism-machine.html (archived at https://perma.cc/ERB9-TT68)

GLOSSARY

@username
The name you choose to represent yourself by on social media. On Twitter it appears shown at the beginning of all your tweets and starts with the @ sign.

1st-degree connections
Direct connections with people you know on a personal level.

2nd-degree connections
Connections to your 1st-degree connections.

3rd-degree connections
Connections to your 2nd-degree connections.

algorithm
A process or set of rules to be followed in calculations or other problem-solving operations, especially by a computer.

Big Data
Very large data sets that may be analysed to reveal patterns, trends and associations, especially relating to human behaviour and interactions.

business timeline/ business page
A business timeline is not a profile. It is a way to promote a business or brand (not an individual) on Facebook through your personal profile. You cannot become friends with a business timeline, you can only Like it.

chatbot
A piece of software that conducts a conversation via text or sound.

clapback
To return a criticism or insult online.

confirmation bias
Preferring information that confirms your own beliefs.

cover photo
A large photo that stretches across the top of your social media profile, like a banner, just above your profile picture. Cover photos will remain public, even if all the rest of your photos are private. Be aware that there are some strict guidelines on the cover photo for your business timeline.

deepfake tech
Used to combine and superimpose existing images and videos on to source images or videos using machine learning.

digital detox
A period of time where someone stops using digital devices and communication platforms.

direct message (DM)
A private message to somebody else on social media.

endorsements	A simpler way of recommending your connections by praising them either for the skills they have on their profile or skills you think they have.
evergreen	Content that doesn't go out of date. It revolves around a topic that's always relevant to readers, regardless of the current news cycle or season.
Facebook personal timeline	Your timeline represents you personally and not as a business. It is your own personal profile, in which people can see a sequence of your activity, photos and wall posts since you joined Facebook. It is a way to share information about yourself with others in order to socialise and network.
fake news	See Chapter 14.
filter bubble	A situation where a person or group of people only encounters information that tends to be consistent with their current beliefs.
follower	Someone who subscribes to your posts. Following you means they will automatically see your posts and updates.
following	Following someone on social media. You automatically see their updates (as much as the algorithms permit).
freemium	A business model whereby basic services are provided free of charge while more advanced features must be paid for.
groups	Usually created by brands, companies, organizations and individuals to drum up support or promote something. You can Like a group and/or become a member of it.
handle	The @username is also sometimes referred to as your handle (an old CB radio term).
hashtag (#)	The # can be used to categorize your content in line with a particular topic. Then someone searching for the topic will see your post.
igtv	A standalone video application by Instagram for Android and iOS smartphones. It allows for longer videos than Instagram.
influencer	A person with the ability to have an effect on others and convince others to buy a specific product, adopt a certain idea or behave in a certain way by promotion or recommendation on social media.
insights	Analytics that show how a user's social media page is performing. Shows interaction, users and reach.
ISM	Internal Social Media activity or platforms.
locking your profile	Allowing only people you follow to see your Twitter updates.

like	If you Like something on a social media page it means that you approve of whatever is being represented, promoted, shown or discussed. You can Like videos, statuses, business pages, people, photos, groups and discussions.
meme	An image, video, piece of text etc, typically humorous, that is copied and spread rapidly by internet users, often with slight variations.
mentions	References to users in other posts by quoting @your username.
notifications	Social media pages notify you with optional messages that let you know if any activity has occurred on your page.
organic social	Using the free tools provided by each social network to build a social community and interact, sharing posts and responding to customer comments.
owned channels	Platforms that a person or company has direct control over (eg website, blog).
page timeline	Appears in browser versions of Facebook and shows milestones since your company or organization was founded.
personal brand	The marketing of people and their careers as brands. It is an ongoing process of developing and maintaining a reputation and impression of an individual, group, or organization.
profile	In your personal profile you can showcase your expertise, skills and recommendations.
profile picture	A small picture that appears on your personal or business profile. It will appear on the site to represent you whenever you comment, post or Like anything on Facebook. Your profile picture on a business timeline is most likely to be your logo or company branding, whereas on your personal timeline it will probably be a picture of you.
retweet (rt)	Used to repeat a specific tweet. It can be used to reiterate what somebody else has said in agreement or to show all your followers a tweet that you are replying to.
sentiment analysis	The process of computationally identifying and categorizing opinions expressed in a piece of text, especially in order to determine whether the writer's attitude towards a particular topic, product etc is positive, negative or neutral.

shitposting	The act of aggressively posting excessive amounts of poor-quality content on social media platforms in order to derail a discussion or provoke a negative response.
SMS	Short message services.
social dashboard	A central place to collect all your social media feeds so that you can manage multiple accounts more effectively (eg hootsuite, Sprout Social).
social media monitoring	Ability to track and analyse conversations happening on social media to help organizations understand audience preferences or sentiment.
status update	Contains information that you want to share with people connected to your Timeline – personal or business-related. The status may contain a picture, link or video.
tagging	Being mentioned in a status update or identified in a picture. You are notified when you have been tagged.
targeted followers	Targeting the people who listen to your tweets for a purpose and following people you want to follow you back.
trends	Popular subjects that are being discussed on social media. Categorised by a hashtag (#).
tweet	A message (maximum length 280 characters) sent via Twitter.
Twitter chat	When a group of users on Twitter connect and converse not by following one another but by following a # around a conversation, eg #tradestalk or #usguys. These are ongoing conversations, often held at a specific date and time each week or month.
Twitter lists	You can sort your followers into segments by creating lists so that you can better organize your Twitter thread.
viral (going viral)	An image, video, or link that spreads rapidly through a population by being frequently shared.
vlog	A video blog or video log. A form of blog for which the medium is video and is a form of web television.
vlogger	Someone who vlogs.

INDEX

Page numbers in *italic* indicate figures or tables.